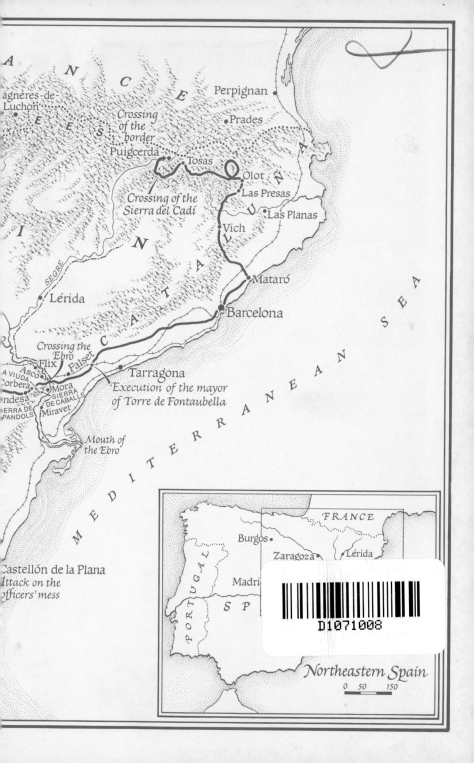

A
N
C
E
P
Y
R
E
N
É
E
S

agnères-de-
Luchon

Crossing
of the
border
Puigcerdá

Tosas

Perpignan

Prades

Olot

Las Presas

Crossing of the
Sierra del Cadí

Las Planas

Vich

SEGRE

Lérida

Mataró

Barcelona

Crossing the
Ebro
Flix   Falset

Asco

A VIUDA
orbera

Mora
SIERRA
DE CABALLS

ndesa

Tarragona

Execution of the mayor
of Torre de Fontaubella

ERRA DE
PANDOLS   Miravet

Mouth of
the Ebro

M E D I T E R R A N E A N   S E A

Castellón de la Plana
Attack on the
officers' mess

FRANCE

Burgos

Zaragoza   Lérida

PORTUGAL

Madrid

SP

D1071008

Northeastern Spain

0   50   150

DARK AND
BLOODY GROUND

DARK AND
BLOODY GROUND

A Guerrilla Diary
of the Spanish Civil War by
Francisco Pérez López

edited and with an introduction by Victor Guerrier
translated by Joseph D. Harris

Little, Brown and Company — Boston – Toronto

Published simultaneously in Canada
by Little, Brown & Company (Canada) Limited

PRINTED IN THE UNITED STATES OF AMERICA

Contents

Contents

INTRODUCTION

Introduction

"COMRADES of the International Brigades! You can go proudly. You are history. You are legend. . . ."

Thus La Pasionaria addressed the foreign volunteers when they were assembled for farewells in Barcelona on November 15, 1938. In accordance with international agreements, they were preparing to leave Spain.

Certain of them chose to remain and return to combat. Until now nothing was known of their fate; nothing of the fate of the prisoners of war; nothing precise concerning the postwar repression; nothing of the guerrilla fighters who were its consequence.

This narrative fills the gap. It is an exceptional historical document. It adds to the legend a final page, a terrible page, written by a twenty-four-year-old guerrilla leader to expose the injustices suffered by the people at the hands of the victors. This testimony is equally exceptional because it is a chapter from a journal kept for the last thirty years by a farm worker of Spanish origin who left France only once, in 1937, to enlist in the armies of the Spanish Republic. It is not just another book. It was not written to be read, and until now it has not been read by anyone. Such singularity confers on the testimony an indisputable authenticity. But this narrative, naïve in form, is also a work of art. The same instinct that enabled its writer as a young man to grasp the fundamental rules of command also gave him an untaught knowledge of how to write.

Having identified the author I think it may be helpful to introduce both him and his work as I came to know them, so that through the starkness of the story the reader may sense the human warmth that is hidden in the genesis of every work of art.

In 1967 I was doing some historical research on the French Revolution, when chance brought me one day to a noble house in a village of Haute-Provence. The head of a very old and illustrious family there graciously opened his archives to me. It was arranged that even in his absence I would have free access to the library which was in a pavilion situated at the end of a garden. I could even work there in the winter; a village woman came each day to tend the fireplace in order to assure the preservation of the books and papers. I could lodge with her better than at the hotel. In the fall I moved in; and that was how I came to know her husband, Francisco, the Spaniard.

He was a day laborer. He hired his services to the landowners of the region — whenever his humor accorded with their needs. This independence was a sign of pride in a man who simply wanted nothing more than to be a farm worker. One of his usual jobs was the surveillance and cultivation of the groves of truffle oaks that were among the principal natural riches of the region. One of my pleasures was to accompany him on his forest rounds.

Francisco was past fifty but had remained spare and sturdy. He walked with a brisk, regular stride whose rhythm never broke for any accident of the terrain. Later on I observed that everything about the man was like the way he walked: his speech, his writing, the firmness of his thought. He was a man who was master of himself.

The luxury of his modest house was its fire, which he tended with care in the big Provençal fireplace from his supply of stumps and tree trunks. Winter is harsh on the high plateaus of Provence. I formed the habit of bringing my papers at the end of the evening to the long table where we ate supper. I worked late into the night, taking advantage of the warmth and companionship around the fire. Francisco's wife would always go to bed first. He would stay up awhile to write his "report."

He had always written down everything he did. It was, he said, an obsession. Each evening he made a summary of the events of the day on a pad. Later he wrote them out, down to the smallest details, in large notebooks. He became very worried when he got behind in his writing. He could not restrict his writing to spare moments alone. When "the urge came over him," the landowners had to wait: he would stay at home writing the whole day. Seeing me work in the quiet of the night, he got into the habit of staying up with me, writing until late at my side at the long table in front of the fire.

He wrote in several notebooks at the same time: one for events, one for a chronology kept in tables, one for accounts and inventories. He was a man of order, who acted with method in everything. His approach delighted my historian's heart: he did not choose among the facts, he reported them all. It is this absence of choice which makes the true journal, more than memoirs, the source of the most precious information for the historian.

When Francisco had closed his notebooks, he would get out a bottle of wine, some bread and some pâté with truffles. We would talk by the fire as we ate.

One evening I told him how I was writing about the origins of the French Revolution. Then, in all simplicity, he revealed that he had written a history of the Spanish revolution. He went to bring me a notebook. At the head of the first page it read: "A study of the political affair in Spain, as seen by Francisco Pérez López, undated, but told according to reality." Then came a draft of a constitution for a new Spanish republic. Then followed a study on the role of guerrillas in a revolutionary action.

With good sense and lucidity he explained to me why a new popular revolution would be impossible in Spain for a long time. He had only written all that from an obsession to write. He had never shown these pages to anyone and had never thought of what might become of them. However, I was sensitive to the respect he seemed to show for them; it was the respect every writer has for a thought expressed, by virtue of which it no longer belongs to him.

These notebooks merited that respect. They were the expression of a dramatic experience. At twenty-one, Francisco had gone from France to Spain to join the armies of the Republic. He fought with the International Brigades on the Ebro, was taken prisoner, and escaped. He got back to France after recruiting and leading a group of guerrillas.

Turning the pages of a notebook, he showed me the beginning of his journal: "Summary of the life of Francisco Pérez López." The epigraph read: "The life of a fighter is never finished; others follow after and bring in the fruits." There followed the story of his family and of his childhood, his entry into Spain, the narratives of the war and captivity. A second notebook told of his escape, the adventures of guerrilla warfare, the return to France, the Resistance, and the battles for liberation, after which began the journal of Francisco, farm worker, written with the same rigor and the same attention.

My first reaction was to have Francisco make arrangements for leaving his notebooks to the Bibliothèque Nationale. The exciting possibility of publishing the part of the journal concerning the war in Spain occurred to me when I learned that there existed no firsthand account of the events of imprisonment and guerrilla war. I told this to Francisco, who left it to me to decide.

His manuscript was written in a form much like that of the journals and memoirs of the seventeenth and eighteenth centuries that I had studied: the same closely written lines running from one edge of the page to the other, without paragraphs, without punctuation. The text was like a thicket; to make it penetrable to the reader it was necessary to open up avenues and place guideposts.

In order to transcribe the journal without altering its spirit, I decided to read several pages each evening. I marked obscure passages, gaps, imprecisions of place and time. Then Francisco and I reread these pages together. Memories came back to him and, quite naturally, the connections were reestablished and the narrative was clarified. In order to respect his spirit and his cadence, I did not take notes! I wrote on the spot, in the light of the memories which we had, as it were, relived together. We worked in that manner all winter.

When I received the typewritten manuscript in Paris, a month after finishing my work, the narrative seemed admirable to me, crystalline in its absolute objectivity. But that was the reaction of an historian. What would be the reaction of a sensitive reader, subjected to the ordeal of violence which is all the harder to bear in that it is not expressed in the narrative, but lurks beneath the surface of the writing on every page? Would not readers expect the author to break the unbearable tension of this unity between narrative and unspoken, ever-present violence, by indulging in the reassuring and familiar devices of subjectivity?

For example, we worked on the terrible evocation of the crossing of the Ebro by the guerrillas. An orphaned child was with them and lost his life there. In the boat carrying them across, Francisco's lieutenant, mortally wounded, found the strength to tell his leader that he, Francisco, was not responsible for the murder of the child. As we read together the page where Francisco had recorded this dramatic episode, he said to me, "When I heard that, my heart was relieved of a great weight." But in his account, Francisco does not say that. Already the enemy was running toward them. It was with his head alone that the leader could save his guerrillas. He had to decide in an instant. And there lies the admirable truth of the account. The man who acts must remain outside all sentiment. Here is the proof that the account was not written for a reader. The author never thought of him for a moment. It is I who think about him now. In delivering this book to the reader, I also deliver Francisco to his judgment.

As we finished editing this episode and sat silently contemplating the fire, Francisco said suddenly, 'Often, in dreams, I see that child again." Nevertheless, I have added nothing to the primary text of the journal. In trying to justify the author, I would betray him. It would require all his admirable naïveté to dare separate at this point the man who acts from the man who suffers.

"Sensitivity is almost never a quality of a man of great genius," wrote Diderot. "He will love justice, but he will exercise this virtue without reaping its sweetness. It is not his heart, but his head, that does all. At the slightest unforeseen circumstance, the sensitive man is lost; he will never be a great king or a great captain. Fill the world of the spectacle with these weepers, but never place one on the stage."

One could not add to Francisco's stripped-down text without altering its truth. The art here is the absence of art. Brice Parain, speaking from experience, has rightly said how for the combatant every word is false. No description is possible; reality for him is the moment of action and is foreign to language. The analysis of the intellectual looking back on it is a lie.

When I reconstructed Francisco's long march on the map and showed astonishment at his detours, he explained that it is much safer for guerrillas to operate on known terrain. That is why Francisco returned as a guerrilla to the regions where he had fought. He told me also that his binoculars had been his best weapon. He only advanced in the open after long observation in which the wind, the sun, and even the flight of birds played their part. In that way he was never surprised: the attack unleashed, he acted without thinking, like an actor who knows his role perfectly. For that reason he never had anything to say about it. Francisco proceeds entirely in the present in his narrative.* If I asked him,

---

*In the English translation the past tense has been used for the sake of smoothness.

he could draw me a plan of the château he attacked. But if I tried to make him develop the "interesting" moments of the narrative, he would swerve away.

One could not add anything to this text, nor could one subtract anything from it. The reader will not fail to be irritated when, once an action is over, the narrator, instead of ceding a moment to feeling, inflicts on the reader his fastidious accounts. Francisco also explained that to me. Guerrilla combat is always a brief action followed by rapid flight in which the guerrilla exhausts his last strength. If he does not regain that strength, he will be in danger. That is why, like an animal, he goes into hiding and sleeps for a long time. Afterwards he eats; hence the importance of provisions. The leader must always have in mind the state of his troop's supplies. Therefore Francisco made his list each evening. He wrote it in cipher on one of those tablets of cigarette paper which in Spain are like thick little books.* That way he always had before his eyes the state of his weapons, provisions, money and tobacco. The latter was more important than one might guess: a smoker deprived of his tobacco is a less effective man. Francisco, a true leader, taught me that the art of command is the art of detail. That is why I did not dare to suppress a single list in what follows. Francisco did in real life what Hemingway has taught us: the author should tell us only of that part of the external world which the consciousness of the hero perceives in the moment the two coincide. After an action Francisco did not cry over his dead;

---

*It was thanks to this book of accounts, which he brought back to France, that Francisco was able to reconstruct his march with so much precision.

he counted the cans of food. When the Ebro was crossed, after rapid good-byes to the wounded lieutenant the guerrillas ran for cover. They waited for the submachine burst announcing that the wounded man had had the strength to kill his enemies, and afterwards the shot announcing his death. Francisco rallied his surrounded troops and took inventory: nothing had been lost, they had so many weapons and ammunition, so much bread, cans and meat. . . . There is the surprising truth of this narrative.

What is important in a work is to be found neither in the story nor in the sources nor in the biography of the author. The essence of the man is hidden in his text. We have seen how his style reveals it. To be properly introduced into the mystery of this work we must see how Francisco's writing reveals to us the secret of a man who at first glance seems to be absent from his work.

The narrative begins with the very Spanish theme of honor, with the "handsome switchblade knife," that rapier of the Spanish people, which Uncle Pedro has the child admire. When one evening his uncle opens the knife full of blood because a watercress merchant has "spoken badly" of Spaniards, Francisco, at the age of six, learns that honor demands that a personal offense be washed away in blood.

Then, in the course of the voyage to Algeria, the theme of justice appears. Francisco discovers the exploitation of man by man. He flees his "exploiter uncles" who want to make him a slave master. In Spain his idealism is nourished by the example of men come from the four corners of the earth to fight for a just cause. Nothing is more moving than the plaint of Francisco after the failure of his efforts to help others in the Forest of Peace:

"How could something so well arranged, something that had made everybody happy, be so quickly destroyed? It seems that those who work for the people can't be with them when they have the chance!"

Again, it is the idealism of Francisco that illuminates the account of his captivity. The fraternity of work seems to triumph over hate, and the narrative is buoyed up by the hope of a reconciliation between victors and vanquished.

Then all at once comes the condemnation. What novelist would not envy the perfection of this composition in which the narrative balances exactly at the central high point of the book. "Before, we had cared about our work and we had been like a family. All that was over. We went back to thinking of our guards as enemies. . . . The spirit of revolution returned." From there until the end, the narrative is swept downward on a tide of vengeance.

It must not be forgotten that the vanquished were the regular soldiers of the legal government of Spain. Coldly the rebel victors, with the complicity of the Church, decreed that these combatants were condemned men under common law. Their chief crime was an error of judgment. But injustice could only engender violence; honor must be cleansed with blood. The guerrillas would execute justice. When the hour of justice sounded, they would all judge together, "like a tribunal marked with the great R of the Republic."

But this young leader of twenty-four years understood that the execution of justice demands integrity. He imposed strict rules on his guerrillas; until the end, no one violated them. The existence the rules meant that even as he unleashed the demons of war, Francisco would always be able to remain their master. It was one of his rarest accomplishments. We will see Francisco, having arrived in view of the frontier with his troop, refuse a politician whom he had set free the easy glory of a last massacre. "I don't kill soldiers," he said; and when the politician mocked him, there was much contempt in Francisco's reply, the contempt of a warrior for the man who, by laughing in front of his victim, loosed all of his demons.

The third theme, that of education, runs through the narrative from childhood on. In the eyes of people kept humble by ignorance, Francisco was "the Frenchman who knows how to read and write." The last message of the terrible dispenser of justice was that before arms, the liberation of man comes through education.

The chevalier de Folard at the same age as Francisco went to learn war with the partisans, as did Montluc and Villars. In 1715 Folard went to Sweden to offer his services to Charles XII. After the king's death, he wrote a summary of the lessons one could draw from the astonishing military career of a prince who won his first victory at the age of eighteen. In conclusion Folard affirmed that war was not a matter of military science but only of innate temperament and a kind of barbaric genius which even a child could possess.

This alliance of "barbaric genius" and temperament is found in Francisco. It made him a fully competent leader on the scale of the action he led. There is no doubt that if the times and the circumstances had cast him into the war at its beginning, he would have attained high command.

The barbaric genius is what has created the legend of El Mexicano (as Francisco was known by his enemies). But it is the temperament, that is to say the sense of balance and measure in his judgments and conduct, that sets apart the Francisco I know. Someday I will try to tell how much I have learned from the example of his life.

In the conclusion to his history of the Spanish revolution, Francisco writes: "Let us find unity and forget the past. Now we look to the future and we can forgive all mistakes even as we speak of them. . . . They belong to a past time."

And thus spoke President Azaña in July 1938 at Barcelona:

"When the torch passes to other hands, to other men, to other generations, let them remember, if they ever feel their blood boil and the Spanish temper is once more infuriated with tolerance, hatred and destruction, let them think of the dead, and listen to their lesson: the lesson of those who have bravely fallen in battle, generously fighting for a great ideal, and who now, protected by their maternal soil, feel no hate or rancor, and who send us, with the sparkling of their light, tranquil and remote as that of a star, the message of the eternal Fatherland which says to all its sons: Peace, Pity and Pardon." *

It is in the light of that truth that all one winter Francisco and I worked to give you this journal. It is in the same light that you must read it.

Victor Guerrier

1969

---

*Hugh Thomas, *The Spanish Civil War* (New York: Harper and Brothers, 1961), pp. 623-624.

MY FRENCH CHILDHOOD

Uncle Pedro

M Y EARLIEST MEMORIES are of Arles, the town in France where after their misfortunes my grandmother and mother came to live with Aunt Francesca, who was married to a former spahi she had met in Oran. I was three years old. They put me in nursery school. That's how I came to speak French before Spanish. Afterwards I went to the grade school on the rue Barbès and learned to read and write. This gave me some importance in the house.

At Almería in Andalucía, where I was born in 1916, my grandfather and his son my father died of the Spanish flu in the same month. My grandmother went half crazy. The doctor told her to move to a new home. That's how she came to France with my mother and me. I was the only man in the family, and the first one of the family to have an education. My grandmother was proud.

For a long time I pretended I didn't understand Spanish so I wouldn't have to do as I was told. But by the time I was six I must have known quite a bit of Spanish because I still remember plenty of stories about my great-uncle Pedro.

One evening he appeared at the house. My grandmother was so happy! She was the oldest in her family, and he was the oldest of the seven brothers. This set them apart from the others. Uncle Pedro was her favorite brother. After he died my grandmother told me his life story because he had been the big man in the family and after my mother I would one day be the head.

He was a baker by trade and a good pastry maker. In Almería he worked right by the inn run by his family. Even when he was young he kept to himself. He went out alone, watched the dances from a distance, drank alone, spoke to no one. But if he saw a child without shoes he'd buy him a pair. He used to give cakes to all the children in the quarter. He was very highly regarded. He met a pretty woman, married her, and moved into a nice house; but it didn't last long. She was silly and flighty. He found out she was deceiving him with the owner of the bakery. He didn't say a word. One evening during mardi gras week she went dancing dressed in a paper costume as they do in Spain. He went to the bakery as usual, but once he got the oven going he went back to the house. He went through the window without a sound. He found his wife asleep, so tired from dancing all evening that she still had on the paper costume. He went and got a can of gasoline, doused the bed and furniture, set fire to the house and returned to his work. He went into the bakery by the back entrance where the cart and wood for the oven were kept. Then he put his bread in the oven. Early in the morning they came to tell him his house had burned down with his wife in it. He acted as if he knew nothing about it. An investigation was made and he was interrogated. They believed his story and he was left to his work.

So he went back to live with his sister. Every evening he would have a drink at the family inn. One night he came in and found three Galicians insulting his two brothers who were waiting on them as they ate and drank. One of the Galicians had even taken out his knife. As the Galicians didn't know Pedro was the older brother they didn't pay any attention to him. He went over and squared the account with slashes of his knife. Two died in the room; the third was wounded but managed to run away. The next day his body was found in a cane field by the side of the road about a quarter of a mile from the inn. His belly was ripped open and he still held his entrails with both hands.

The police arrested the whole family. Pedro pleaded self-defense. It didn't work. He was sentenced to life imprisonment; but during his transfer from Almería to Barcelona he escaped by jumping off the moving train. He sailed to Algeria and took refuge with his other brothers, successful colonialists who already did a big business exporting vegetables to France. They arranged for some fake papers and got Pedro a job in a bakery in the Jewish quarter. But he often drank a lot and one day he fell asleep on a bench in the square. When he woke up it was night and an Algerian was in the process of stealing his watch and his money. Pedro pulled out his knife and bled the thief like a chicken, leaving the body on the bench. Then he went to his brother Luis who put him on the first boat to France. That's how he came to us.

I can see him still: tall, thin, dressed like a peasant in a corduroy suit and black hat, with flashing eyes, a small mouth and big hands and feet. He spoke very seldom or not at all, only to answer questions from his beloved sister.

He found work in the bakery across from the department store Galeries de Paris. He was very kind to me. He brought me little buns and in the evenings he would show me his handsome switchblade knife.

He would drink anywhere, but most often he went to the Bar des Amis. One evening he came home and sat down as usual. Then he took out his knife and opened it. It was covered with blood. He calmly asked his sister to wash it in hot water. My grandmother did as he asked, but when she returned it to him all clean she gave him a good piece of her mind, saying it was always like that when people went out drinking. Uncle answered that he was free to go drink where he pleased but he didn't like it when people spoke ill of Spaniards.

He had been having his drink as usual in the Bar des Amis. A watercress peddler who was already drunk insulted him, spoke badly of Spaniards, and then tried to make him pay for a round. Uncle Pedro said nothing, paid for the round, and left. When he got outside he walked along the boulevard a way and hid behind a plane tree. He waited. When the peddler came out drunk he followed him and at the corner of the bridge he took him by surprise, cutting his throat and flinging his body into the canal.

I was sitting at the table doing my homework and heard the whole story. Uncle Pedro put his knife back in his pocket, then came over and sat quietly beside me. For once he was smiling. He smoked a cigarette and then went to bed, as he had to report for work at the local bakery at midnight.

He worked there for a month. Then he left again for Algeria. After a couple of months he got sick, and came back to stay with us. We put him in the hospital to be cared for; when he was better he went back to work at the bakery again. Then he took it into his head to go back to Algeria. A while later my grandmother received a letter saying he had died in a hospital there. He had stayed fierce to the end and refused help from his brothers.

My Grandmother

M Y GRANDMOTHER inherited the family fortune: an inn and some land at the edge of Almería. Every six months great-uncle Tonin sent her the income from the property. But it was in herself that my grandmother had her real fortune; wherever she was, money flowed to her like water.

By profession she was a tailor and my mother was a seamstress. When they moved to Arles they quickly managed to find work making shirts and clothes for men, women and children. These were commissioned by a good store, the Galeries de Paris.

My grandmother communicated with the merchants as best she could, as much with gestures as with words. But for important affairs she liked to take me along so she wouldn't be cheated, since she could neither read nor write. That's why she always took me with her when she went to buy fabrics. The salesgirl unrolled the bolts and made the cloth snap. My grandmother wet her finger and felt the material. No one needed to tell her anything. She'd say no, the salesgirl would get another roll, and soon there was a whole pile. Then all of a sudden my grandmother would say yes, this one has the right texture. Then they would discuss the price and my grandmother had me repeat in Spanish everything the salesgirl said.

We would return to the house with a big bolt. My grandmother would unroll it on a big table. I held the order from the Galeries de Paris as I was the only one in the house who knew how to read. She would ask, "What size?" She had such a sure eye for her work that she never took measurements. With chalk she drew a line and crossed it with another, in one motion, without a ruler. She did the same for the shoulders and collar. Then she took the scissors and snip, snip, she cut with such great strokes it frightened me. Then my mother would sew all night, and I would feel proud to see the coats and pants in the store window.

But cutting cloth didn't take up all my grandmother's time, and as she could never sit still doing nothing, she went into business. At that time* there were not many Spanish products available in the markets. So my grandmother wrote to Uncle Tonin, and all kinds of things began coming to us via an agent in Marseille. So as not to draw attention, everything was sent in small cartons weighing about fifty pounds. Each time that M. Maisonvieille, who had a deluxe horsedrawn taxi, went to the station with a client he returned with a carton. There

---

*1926: Francisco was ten years old. V.G.

were spices, Spanish nougat, dried meats, wine gourds and even brooms. My grandmother had also found a Spanish sausage maker in Montpellier. Each week he sent a package of longaniza blanca, butifarva, sobresada, chorizo, etremeno, montiza, etc. That wasn't enough. From Marseille the Luis Malla firm sent cases of salted fish of all kinds every week: tuna, cavallo, melva, English codfish, dried fish eggs, herring filets, pickled herrings, pressed sardines, olives and canned goods of all kinds. The house was a real store. I translated the letters and invoices of the merchants into Spanish. I wrote lists of everything and my grandmother marked them with crosses and circles and squares and signs of her own and managed her accounts quite well.

On market day the peasants came to trade. We lived on the ground floor of a big house and the courtyard was ours. On market day there were so many people in it you couldn't move. The peasants brought eggs, cheeses, rabbits, chickens, guineas and even little lambs and kids. You hardly knew where to walk. On the other days of the week, my grandmother had a woman, Mme. Decamp, who sold our goods every morning in the little market. None of this merchandise was ever declared and we never paid taxes on it. We were rolling in money from all this commerce as well as the clothes making. Then my mother met Juan Morillo, a Catalan who earned thirty francs and two liters of wine a day working in the fields. They lived together and got on very well. Uncle Juan was very kind to me. He gave me pennies for Sunday. He wore wooden shoes and had a big moustache that turned white in the winter when it froze outside.

Once in a while we were visited by the police. The superintendent would ask my grandmother what all this merchandise was for. My grandmother would answer half in French, half in Spanish, "Eh! I've got many things. See all this cloth? It's for my work."

"But Madame Antonia," the superintendent would say, "all these sausages aren't for your work."

"Eh! Monsieur le commissaire, I must think of my family. I have nine children."

My grandmother always spoke as though all my uncles from Algeria were about to come to the house. Then she'd roll up some sausages in a paper and slip them in the superintendent's pocket and he'd go off saying, "Madame Antonia, this is the last time . . ." And when he returned three months later it was the same thing all over again, and again it was "the last time."

What the superintendent didn't know was that my grandmother now made sausages herself. She bought the leftovers from Michel's butcher shop at reduced prices. She sent me to the slaughterhouse at night with cans that I'd bring back full of blood, along with a package of entrails. The rest of the night we made all sorts of sausages, including Spanish blood sausages.

It's not surprising that with this kind of life I was the worst pupil in school. Grammar and arithmetic never got into my head. But I was very good at drawing; that meant everything to me. In the spring I often skipped school to explore the countryside. I would pick fruit and look for birds' nests and sleep for hours under the trees, and I would come home all dirty and often got a whipping. But that didn't bother me. Still, I had good teachers, Monsieur and Madame Bureau. They were very patient and they loved their profession. I have never forgotten them.

24

First Jobs

AT FOURTEEN I was put in another school, the one behind the town hall. I stayed there two years doing
nothing. Then I entered the trade school. There I found
I had talent for machinery, foundry work and joinery. I
was a star in mechanical drawing. After a year of school,
I was able to get work at the shipyard where my uncle
the spahi was a foreman. My job was heating rivets. I
soon got tired of that and left after three months. I tried
a different trade, first as apprentice pastry baker and
then as chef's helper at the Grand Hotel. After a while I
went back to the shipyard, but this time as an apprentice mechanic. I was paid well: 1.75 francs an hour.
When bonuses for piecework were added to that, it
came to what for me was a lot of money.

At that time what I enjoyed most was getting an occasional job as an extra whenever a troupe of actors came
to the theater. I would wear a fine costume to play a
baron who chased the ladies, for instance, or carry a staff
like the beadles in church and tap on the stage to an-
nounce: the Marquis So-and-so. But I couldn't resist
making faces to get laughs from the audience.

Then there was the circus. Once the great Pinder
Circus came to town. My friends and I walked around

the tent looking for a place where we could slip under the canvas without paying to get in. But they had two big Negroes patrolling the tent watching for gate-crashers. One evening I managed to get in and went up to a man sitting in the reserved section. I said, "I think you have my seat. Could I see your ticket?" He gave it to me and I said I would take it to the ticket window and check. Then I walked around a bit and sat down in an empty seat. But one of the big Negroes noticed me. He came over with an employee who asked if I had a ticket. I took it out and they were both astonished. Later as I went out I was stopped by the two Negroes, who took me to the manager. He smiled and said, "You're quite a comedian. Since you love the circus, I'll give you a job if you like." "Doing what?" I asked. He replied I would learn to be a clown. That pleased me very much. He asked where I lived and the next day he came to see my grandmother. She howled in protest: I was her only son (she always called me her son), she wanted to keep me home, she needed me. . . . The director left, but that evening I went to see him and told him that I could go. Then I told my mother that the shipyard was sending me to Arles for a while to repair barges. The next day I left with the circus.

I traveled in a beautiful trailer with three clowns who taught me the trade. We did not have to help set up the tent. As soon as we arrived we practiced our roles. First they taught me how to take slaps. Usually the slaps are for fun and you make the noise by clapping your hands together. But they dealt me real slaps and I made a funny grimace. That was just what they wanted: it was the only way to learn to make a real grimace. It was the same with falling off a bench. First they had me sit on a bench, then without warning, they shoved me off, hard. I hurt myself falling and got up bent double with pain. Again that was what they wanted; my contortions were natural. Then they taught me to fall, throwing my elbows out behind at just the right moment. Then it was falling on my head, covering it with my arms at the last moment to protect it. Finally we rehearsed a number. Once we knew it well, always making the same gestures, the same grimaces and saying the same words, there was nothing to doing it before the public. I made people laugh and was a great success. The director was very pleased. We traveled around France for a month. But when the circus went to Marseille to embark for South America, I left it and went back home.

This adventure made me a celebrity in my friends' eyes. They were not the flower of the town. With them I had become a steady customer of the local whorehouses. I knew all the girls. Sometimes their pimps would even ask me to place girls for them in Nîmes, Arles, Aix or Marseille. The police started keeping an eye on me.

At that time the Spanish Republic was beginning its propaganda campaign to get young Spaniards in France to enlist in the army. I could see myself in helmet and bandolier. That didn't appeal to my grandmother. To change my mind, she decided that the whole family would leave for Algeria to visit my successful great-uncles there.

Voyage to Algeria

WE GOT OUR PASSPORTS and embarked on the *Sidi-Brahim*. The sea was rough; most of the passengers were seasick. We debarked at Oran and took the train for Sidi-bel-Abbès.

There Grandmother quickly found a little house to rent not far from the quarter where great-uncle Ramón lived. He was an unpleasant and domineering man. He was very rich yet he always wore dirty clothes spotted with grease and streaked with flour. His wife was small and spiteful; she despised the Algerians. They had a daughter and two sons. The oldest son, Ramón, was a fighter and a drinker. The other, Manuel, was funny in the head. He had been in the Spanish Foreign Legion. He played the accordion, his fingers covered with rings. He was always laughing, but he was a liar. He worked in his father's bakery.

Great-uncle Ramón owned a flour mill, four bakeries, a hotel on the boulevard and several large farms outside the town. He lived in the Negro quarter above one of his bakeries. He hired me and I worked with his son and daughter. Uncle Ramón had a stand in the main square where he sold his bread. In the mornings his daughter would make the rounds of the town with a cart full of bread and I, the nephew, would go with her. She was eighteen, a liar, and a flirt, spoiled by money. Our route went by Uncle Ramón's hotel. It was run by two sisters. I got along fine with one of them, a pretty brunette of twenty. But my cousin was jealous and would always find a reason not to let me leave the cart to deliver the bread to the hotel. Afternoons I worked at the bakery with Manuel, meaning he made me do all the work, weighing the dough, preparing the oven and cleaning up while he played the accordion. That made me mad, especially since he always played the same tunes. I was paid only ten francs a day even though I was their nephew, and they didn't count overtime.

Uncle Ramón ran a bakery in another quarter of the town and two of great-uncle Manuel's sons ran the other two.

Before coming to Algeria, great-uncle Ramón had gone to seek his fortune in Argentina. First he'd been a baker, then a traffic cop. After a few years he'd gotten sick because of the climate, so he'd rejoined his brothers in Algeria. They'd helped him. Now he was one of the richest bakers in the town. But he was very bad to the workers, didn't pay much, and mistreated the Algerians. He always carried a revolver with a bullet in the chamber ready to fire. He knew he was hated by the people. He was always sickly; he couldn't eat as he liked and was forbidden to drink at all.

My other great-uncle in Sidi-bel-Abbès, Manuel, was very nice. In the upper quarter above the station beyond the big esplanade, he had a large bakery with lots of gardens around the building and a farm where at least thirty Algerians worked the land and raised poultry and horses. I went to see him as often as I could. He was a great guy. He fed me, took me out in his car and showed me a good time, giving me plenty of money to spend. He liked to go on a binge, drink and run after loose women, while his oldest son looked after the bakery. We would come in late at night and I'd sleep at his house. He was like a father to me and wanted me to live with him. Despite his faults he was good to the poor Algerians. He was liked by everyone, which was very rare for a Spanish colonialist in the region of Oran.

After a while my grandmother decided to go visit the other uncles. She took me with her. My mother stayed in Sidi-bel-Abbès with Juan, her Catalan common-law husband, who worked here and there around the city.

One day we took the train to visit Uncle Antonio, a big landowner who lived far away in the mountains by Tlemcen. We left in the morning and didn't get there until afternoon the next day. The heat was fierce. We got off at a little station in the middle of mountains covered with oak forests. We were going down to the plain when all at once we saw an immense farm with vineyards, fruit trees, gardens and fields of grain. My grandmother told me Uncle Antonio owned all this. The land was his as far up the mountain as you could see. What a sight that farm was! It was a regular village with a bakery and everything, and Uncle Antonio himself ensconced in a palace surrounded by gardens. He was a bachelor, but I soon realized that he had an Algerian mistress. She served his meals and they slept together.

We spent three days visiting his fields, his plantations and his mountains. We saw between three and four hundred workers. My great-uncle usually spoke softly and he always drank moderately, but when he gave orders he was very firm and underlined his words with his hands. At each step people came to greet us. There were storehouses everywhere. It was like an anthill, there were so many people bringing in merchandise, vegetables and fruits and others leaving with boxes ready for shipment. Goods went out by truck, muleback, horse cart, and some even by camel trains headed for the south.

We stayed twenty-one days and lived like royalty. My great-uncle wanted to keep me with him. He told me, "I am old, you are young. I have no one. You'll get used to living like me with these Algerian Moors. I provide food for them and they make me rich." When the time came for us to go, we embraced like brothers and even cried at parting. He gave us lots of presents. We returned to Sidi-bel-Abbès in one of his trucks taking back oil, perfumes, fruits, hams and Spanish sausages. Anything my grandmother showed a liking for he gave her at once. He also gave her a large sum of money.

Uncle Antonio had become a powerful colonialist, but he was also loved like a pasha.

We stayed home awhile to rest from that fine trip. Then my grandmother and I went to visit Uncle Luis at Pérugnot, a town between Oran and Sidi-bel-Abbès, where he had settled when he first left Spain.

He lived in a fine house on a wide street. He was tall and slender, and dressed very correctly. His wife was much younger than he. They had at the time only one child, a girl of twelve.

On both sides of the house there were storehouses full of goods. My uncle owned almost the whole street and in addition had four immense plantations where he grew oranges, artichokes, etc. He was always making the rounds of the town looking after the departures and arrivals of his trucks. He came and went in the bars, drinking constantly. He had to have his ten to fifteen anisettes before each meal. He was very serious and never laughed. He always yelled his orders. He didn't pay his workers much and he was always insulting them and treating them like shirkers. He wanted me to stay with him to supervise the merchandise. But they didn't know when to stop working in Algeria!

We stayed a week. When we left, he didn't even bother to leave the bar where he was drinking.

We took the train back to my other Uncle Manuel's, in Oran. By evening we were with him in his house on the place Bastrand. Right away I saw we didn't have to worry about our lodgings. The house was huge; there were at least fifteen unused rooms, all furnished.

Uncle Manuel was no taller than average; he was a bit on the heavy side (the only one in the family with a big figure) and had no hair on his head. At home he was gentle, but outside he acted authoritarian, always speaking as though in anger. Then he would come in and laugh to himself at seeing the workers run. Besides the warehouses on the square he had others down at the docks.

He was constantly receiving goods from his brothers and others. Trucks unloaded, goods were put in crates and sacks, then other trucks were loaded and taken to the port for shipment. Uncle Manuel's son directed the branch warehouse in Marseille. The family goods were unloaded there and sent all over France and beyond. I never went to see the son even when I lived in Marseille later on. Besides his warehouses Uncle Manuel had garages, houses, stores, a hotel, villas at the seaside and even a yacht for fishing and taking his friends out.

He was married to a woman of about the same age as himself. Besides the son in Marseille they had a daughter who was then nineteen. She was so proud you couldn't go near her. A lazy, good-for-nothing princess. All day long she strolled along the seashore with friends of the same sort. They would have been ashamed to speak to Algerians, and even to Spaniards.

Uncle Manuel's motto was everything for himself, nothing for others. He yelled all the time and paid little for many hours' work. His standing was never certain; one day he would make a great deal, another nearly nothing. It depended on the ships.

He offered me a job supervising the trucks. I'd have to work all kinds of hours, even at night, but I would be well paid and well fed. I didn't want to do it; I couldn't stand his daughter. We stayed only two days and then got back on the train for Sidi-bel-Abbès.

To make a complete round of the family we would have had to visit Uncle Tonin too. He was the youngest of the brothers. But he was the only one who had stayed in Spain to look after my grandmother's affairs. According to her stories and the reports of people who came from Almería to France, he was of middle height, lean and had white streaks in his hair. He was lively, but heartless. He was married to a big, fat, very domineering woman. They had one son.

Uncle Tonin supervised all the property: the inn that had now become a big hotel with a garage, the fields, the vineyards, the olive orchards. He sent his sister, my grandmother, the income from the property from 1920 until 1934, five thousand pesetas every six months. But after our return from Algeria we didn't receive any more. His son had made a career of the army after going to school at Zaragoza. During the war he joined Franco's side and was a captain in the Civil Guard.* When my grandmother learned I wanted to join the Republican army, she told me not to let my identity be known. He might kill me so as to keep all the inheritance for himself even though there were signed documents saying that my grandmother was the sole heir.

After visiting all the uncles we found ourselves back in Sidi-bel-Abbès. Juan worked some but most of the time he was in jail. Fortunately we had a good reserve of money. I worked from time to time for Uncle Ramón. But Francesca was always trying to pick a fight with me. Sundays I took my little nephews to the movies; they spoke Algerian. In the evening I went to the dance near the Foreign Legion barracks.

There was a gang of Spaniards' sons in my quarter. They had fun beating up Algerian boys and also those like myself that they called "the French Spaniards." Soon I always carried my switchblade on Sundays. I kept it up my sleeve for fear of being searched. It was held in place by a rubber band.

One evening I came home contentedly. I was happy because I had a new girl friend, a pretty Spanish brunette who sold ice cream. I was walking along thinking of her

---

*The Civil Guard was a national police force organized like an army — led by a general and officers with military rank. Members never served in their home provinces and had a deserved reputation for ruthlessness. (Thomas, *The Spanish Civil War*, p. 48.) Trans.

when I encountered the gang. The leader, the oldest and huskiest, began insulting me. He came nearer while his four pals laughed at his taunts. Suddenly he threw a punch which hit my shoulder and he started to swing at my head. At this moment I let the knife fall from my sleeve with a quick jerk. The punch got me in the stomach. I fell but had time to stab him in the belly. When I got up his pals saw the knife covered with blood. They ran off leaving their leader writhing in pain on the ground. He cried and begged my forgiveness. Feeling pity, I helped him get up and supported him as we walked to his house. Fortunately the wound didn't seem too bad. Then I went to bed. I was a little nervous, but I slept peacefully. Nevertheless, the next day I decided to leave for Oran.

I had a little pocket money so I rented a room at a cheap hotel in the old port. As in Spain, each room had a door opening onto an interior courtyard, but there were no windows. For light there was only an oil lamp, but the room was very clean and the bed was good. I left my key with the landlady; she fixed everything up for me and I went out for a walk. I soon ate up my money. The landlady's husband, a fisherman, introduced me to some fishing boat owners. I started to work and earned quite a bit. Mornings from two to six I unloaded the fish crates. Then I picked fish out of the nets and helped clean up the boats. I did three or four boats every morning, and for each boat I got a crate of fish. I took them to a dealer who gave me ten francs for each crate. Two or three times a week I'd smuggle a dozen cartons of cigarettes onto one of the big boats. The customs men knew me; we often drank together.

Three brothers from Martinique lived in the room next

to mine at the hotel. Their sister, a seventeen-year-old mulatto, chocolate colored but very pretty, lived in a room on the other side. She did housework for a captain in the Foreign Legion. I became good friends with the brothers. I gave them cigarettes, cigars, tobacco and even cheap brandy that the dockers swiped for me from the holds of the ships. Soon Lolita, the sister, came to my room every evening. She was happy. The owners of the hotel often asked us for supper. The fisherman and I brought lots of fresh fish to the hotel.

It was 1936. Things were beginning to stir in Spain. And the memory of all my exploiter uncles was beginning to bother me badly. I didn't want to have anything more to do with them and one day I went to the Spanish consul to get papers to go to Republican Spain. But by the time I got the papers there weren't any more boats. I had just missed the last one — fortunately, it turned out, as it was captured by the Nationalists. I hoped for another chance. While I waited I got a job on a fishing boat.

We smuggled as much as we fished. The steamers all carried life-saving rafts. Some were made with a big balloon divided in quarters. When you blew it up it made a balloon a yard in diameter. The sailors smuggling on board the steamer tied their packages to the balloons. When the ship came in sight of the coast where we were waiting in our boat, they threw the whole thing into the sea behind them. It fell in the wake where we followed. We had only to pull up the goods. Then we put a layer of paper on the bottom of the crates, arranged the merchandise, spread another layer of paper, put our fish on top, and went into port to unload. We always had a rifle on board. But not for firing on the customs agents: if their motorboat came in sight, we fired the rifle at the balloons and everything disappeared into the water. Once we even had to sink a boat. No matter! The boss earned big money and he quickly replaced it. When there was an especially big deal, we gave the customs agents a share. It was safer.

One day I ran into my mother in one of the town squares. My grandmother had guessed my intentions and sent her to look for me. Money had begun falling in value; we had to go back to France. Everything was arranged for our embarkment on a handsome modern transatlantic liner, the *Sidi-bel-Abbès*.

Departure for Spain

WE FOUND OURSELVES back in Arles, almost broke but all in good health. My grandmother got credit everywhere and took up her clandestine business. My mother started her dressmaking again and Uncle Juan went back to working on the farms.

I spent several weeks doing nothing. Then, with forty francs in my pocket, I left for Marseille. I got a room in the old port and I looked for work unloading fishing boats as in Oran. But I was paid only a few fish; sometimes I couldn't even buy a drink.

In my garret it was impossible to sleep. The whores went up and down the stairs all night with their clients. Then there were fights, and the police busted in almost every night. Luckily I found a good job at the wholesale market. I helped unload the trucks in the early morning. I became known. I had my own clients and did pretty well. I ate in the kitchen of a bar called Prosper's and never had to pay. In the afternoons I went to play cards at the Palmtrees Bar on the old port. The owner was an Englishman. He had an adopted daughter, a very pretty, very serious, Japanese girl. As I was always talking with her he hired me as a waiter.

Sing-la had beautiful almond eyes; she was slender but she had a lovely bosom. I went down for coffee with milk every morning. She served it to me along with two croissants and a pack of Gitane cigarettes with a hundred-franc note slipped inside. That was a lot; in those days a laborer made forty francs a day. My job wasn't really to wait on the bar but was something easier and more fun. Three nights a week, starting at ten, I had to play cards at the table near the telephone booth. I wasn't to take my eyes off the bar when new customers arrived. If after serving them the bartender picked up a yellow envelope and held it a moment in his hand, it was the signal. Then the customer, sometimes two or three of them, went to the telephone booth. As soon as they closed the door I pressed a button at the foot of the table on my left. The booth was an elevator and it took the regulars to the basement where there were opium, gaming tables, roulette and prostitutes. I stayed there until four in the morning. Then I went upstairs to bed, and Sing-la, whose room was next to mine, often came to sleep with me.

Her father the Englishman liked me a lot. He wanted me to marry her and so did she. But I smelled danger. Once a week the boss sent me off to deliver little packets to rich people's houses in Marseille. They gave me good tips. I always had pockets full of bills. I was dressed well: soft hat, cravat, deluxe shoes, and when I had nothing to do I was always with my little Japanese who adored me.

One day I decided to go see my parents and take them a bit of money. The next day, a Sunday, I went for a walk in the town. I hadn't gone a hundred yards when some policemen stopped me and told me to go to the station with them. There they questioned me, insulted me and put me in jail. I was there two days, still not knowing why. Then they took me back to the station and let me go with all sorts of excuses and little smiles. But I had received two terrific slaps from the inspector, my hat was punctured and my cravat was torn.

Shaken, I stayed at home a few days to get myself together. I was even sick in bed for a day. One morning at four there was a loud knocking on the door: the police, tommy guns in hand. They gave me just enough time to dress and then took me off in the Black Maria. There was a fever in the air at the station. They interrogated me: you were with the others, it was you who fired, etc. They shoved, slapped and punched me without giving me a chance to answer. Then I was led off to jail between two gendarmes with revolvers in their hands. I tried to protest. Then the two gendarmes really started beating me up. It went on like that for four days. I thought of the capers in Marseille. But no! It had happened at Arles. A smuggling job. A car had gone through a barricade and a gendarme had been mortally wounded. They finally caught the killer, so they let me go, again with excuses and smiles. But that didn't undo the blows, the insults and the days without food.

I stayed a few more days, spending the nights making the rounds of all the brothels. But I'd had enough of all that. Soon I would be called up for military service. Better to go to the war in Spain than to the barracks. One evening I told my parents I was going to the movies. I made the rounds of the bars and told the girls my plans. Right away they loaded my pockets. I went to the station and took the train for Puigcerdá. Then I got off and crossed the border on foot. At the first Spanish guardpost I reported my illegal entry. When I said I had come to join the Republican army they congratulated me. They had me fill out a large form to take with me.

I took the train to Barcelona. It was December 1937.

WAR IN SPAIN

March—November, 1938

With the Commando Unit of the XVth International Brigade

By 17 March 1938, when the Nationalist forces under General Dávila had entrenched themselves at Aragón, Francisco had arrived in Spain to join the XVth International Brigade. The Internationals had retreated from Caspe (which was taken on 17 March) as far as the Ebro. At Gandesa on the Ebro they held off the Nationalists for several days, performing what Hugh Thomas described (The Spanish Civil War) as "prodigies of valor" in order to allow the Republican army to evacuate its men and material and to regroup beyond the river.

This section of the Ebro, about sixty miles from its mouth, was to play an important part in Francisco's story. He first came to this region in April and May with the XVth Brigade to attempt to capture Gandesa. Evacuated after being wounded on 17 September, Francisco returned a month later to help defend the same part of the Ebro, in an effort to contain the Nationalist counteroffensive. It was there that he was taken prisoner.

V. G.

AT BARCELONA as soon as I got off the train there was an alert. Bombs fell. I couldn't leave the station. I went into the shelter, a large underground tunnel, and

43

showed my paper to the man in charge. He assigned me a little room with a bed, table, chair, blanket and sheet. I was lucky; everyone else, children, women, men, slept every which way in the corridors. I was already being treated like a soldier. In the room the light burned all night. I covered the bulb with a little sack of blue paper. But I couldn't sleep anyway. All night long there were knocks on the door; people wanted to come in and sleep on the floor as there wasn't any more room in the corridors. So I decided to leave the door open; that way a whole family could sleep on the floor rolled up in blankets.

In the morning, the man in charge of the shelter gave me the room key. I went to the Recruits' Barracks. I showed them my paper. Right away a captain took me into an office. There he gave me a card. It had numbers written all around the edges; in the middle it said: *Permiso d'Estado Mayor.* With this card, he explained, I could eat every day in any of the barracks in Barcelona and would get the same rations as the soldiers of the International Brigade. Every morning at nine o'clock I had to present myself for roll call at the Recruits' Barracks; there I would be given a pack of tobacco.

The captain took me from one office to another. I passed my medical test after being weighed, measured, and examined. I was politely questioned in the offices of the International Brigade. I explained how I'd entered the country; they were very pleased. They gave me all the necessary papers: a special pass good at any time, a ration card, papers for drawing pocket money. When I left at eleven o'clock, I had my pockets full with three packs of cigarettes and five thousand pesetas, and I had free passage in all of Republican Spain.

I looked for a room. I found one at Pueblo Nuevo, not far from the Spartacus Barracks. I went there for lunch at eleven and for dinner at five in the evening: a *surco* (roll), a bowl of soup, a plate of beans, and dessert, usually an orange.

As I didn't know anyone, I went for walks. The enemy planes bombed every two hours; the bombs fell all over. I ate at the first barracks I came to, usually the Karl Marx, beside the zoo. I also went to a Basque bar, near the post office, the Achourie. There I'd drink a pitcher of wine and a glass of vermouth. I bought a lot of roasted nuts. I had a good time. Mornings, after roll call I'd go to the beach. The fishing boats were coming in. I ate a lot of grilled sardines. Then I would go to a nightclub in the Barrio Chino that was called Les Françaises. Most of the women there were French. I talked with them, smoked, etc. I went to the movies. I also knew a coffee bar where they sold Mexican powdered milk and *churros*. It was always packed.

This easy life lasted a month. I'd formed habits and made friends. One morning at the roll call they ordered me to step out. I left the line; they put me to one side along with two or three hundred other volunteers. They took us to a large room. We undressed and showered. Then we were each given a shirt, pants, jacket and sweater, all khaki, very good cloth. Then a cap with a red pompom and a belt with a bandolier to go over the shoulder. Then insignia: to sew on the left shoulder, a star with five red points; for the right shoulder, a skull and crossbones. Then they gave us each a big box containing another khaki uniform of lighter color and more ordinary cloth, a spoon, a fork, a canteen, two sheets, a blanket, a poncho, a metal plate, another belt, a lighter cap, five packages of cigarettes, two small bags of American tobacco and, strangely, a very nice pipe. Finally there were a small rucksack and a backpack. All this packed in a box, and all clothes the right size. The boxes were tied with a special heavy cord and had a label attached. Mine read: 1ST COMPANY, XVTH INTERNATIONAL BRIGADE, 1ST DEATH PLATOON, 35TH DIVISION.

As soon as we were dressed we put the boxes on our backs and loaded them onto a truck marked with the insignia of the XVth Brigade.

Then we went back into the hall. We were given a fine pair of shoes and a pair of socks, which we put on right away. All our old civilian clothes were put on a pile in the middle of the room. In my new jacket I had the pipe, a bag of tobacco, two packages of cigarettes and four boxes of matches. As we went out, a commander gave each of us a large paper. It said we had to be at the "France" station to take the train at one o'clock.

We all went for a walk and saw our girls for the last time. At eleven we were at the Karl Marx Barracks for lunch. Some officers came and ate with us, and we talked as friends. I noticed that like us they had the skull insignia on their right shoulders, while a lot of the other officers and soldiers didn't. Intrigued, I questioned the captain eating next to me. He replied that those who wore this insignia were part of a special unit assigned to preparation for the big attacks. He said, "Don't get upset, it's only given to those who can take care of themselves on their own."

After lunch I went to the station. A military train was waiting for us. They called the roll and we got on. At two we left for an unknown destination. The train stopped at several stations where names of soldiers ordered to that destination were called out. Then we left and the next time the train stopped we were in the country. We got out and were taken to a big mansion, probably an old château. Everything there was ready for us. We ate well and went to sleep on iron beds: I was tired and I slept well. The next day, very early, we got back on the train. At Olot, a little town near the French border, we switched from the train to trucks which took us to the church of a little village, Las Presas. There we found our boxes which the trucks had brought from Barcelona. In the church were a row of beds on each side with a space between. Roll was called; each soldier was given a number corresponding to the number of his bed and nothing was left to do but bring in the boxes. I didn't go with the rest. I understood that there were two companies of three platoons each as well as the officers of general staff. I was taken two hundred yards away to a farm. An officer introduced me to the farmer who took me up to the third floor. Surprise — there were sixteen beds, a handsome cupboard for each, a long table, two big benches and two chairs, one at each end. The farmer was very kind. He had a wife and two daughters, twenty-two and twenty-five years old. There were also four young women in uniforms each with a white armband and a red cross. I asked the officer if I was supposed to go eat with the others at the church. No; he left me with the farmer, who took me downstairs to the kitchen where there was a table loaded with enough food for the whole platoon.

The men in the platoon at the church were drilling. I

went to watch them march; they had new rifles, grenades and ammunition. They marched in ranks of three. I sat on a rock and watched their maneuvers. Then I went for a walk. At twelve I went back to the farm for dinner. The women soldiers and the farmer's family were there. We all ate together. We had lots of meat, ham, fruit; afterwards coffee, cognac, and a cigar. We talked about this and that; the farmer's two daughters were next to me. I told them stories and they laughed heartily. In the afternoon my box was brought to me. I put my things in the cupboard and made my bed. I'd been given two towels and soap. Then I went for a walk in the country. Then it was supper and afterwards I went straight to bed. I was alone in the big room. Early in the morning, one of the farmer's daughters brought up coffee with milk, bread and butter. About nine, I was called for breakfast in the kitchen. I took all I wanted from the table and went back up to my room to eat, carrying a jug of wine with me.

Later in the morning a truck came to the farm. Fifteen men got out. On their uniforms they wore the same insignia I did. They greeted me. They were all veterans; they spoke English. I spoke French to them and nearly all of them answered in French. There was a big blond devil, a Dutchman. Another was very small, you'd say a kid of sixteen; he was a Czech. I led them upstairs. Each one took a bed and a cupboard. One of them took out a harmonica and started playing. Very well, too; he was Swiss. I asked who the leader was. They said, "There isn't one. We are all leaders. When the enemy appears we'll see the worth and courage of each man, and the best one will be leader." On one side of my bed I had the Dutchman, on the other, Hotto, a blond Englishman, who was always smiling and spoke very correct French.

At noon the four women brought us lunch. There was too much to eat and too much to drink. We ate like lions, laughing, singing, talking. Some told their stories. Only one remained quiet and sad, the Czech.

On the third day the captain of the Christopher Columbus Barracks arrived. He came into the room and greeted us. He brought us our arms, a whole truckload. There were a box full of knives, daggers, and bayonets, a radio transmitter, maps, and textbooks on war. Then he had us assemble in the courtyard and gave us a political speech. Afterwards he gave me a list of the names of the comrades, along with their assignments. So I learned a lot about each one.

Then the captain proceeded with the election of a leader for the platoon. I was elected. But I was elected not for my military merit but because I was the only one who could read, write and speak Spanish as well as French. That made it simpler for the general staff.

We selected three group leaders.

The big Dutchman would be my courier. Then the captain ate with us, and before leaving gave me the orders from the general staff of the brigade.*

My platoon of sixteen men was a good one; it was made up of good comrades and especially of good

---

*From 1938 on, the International Brigades' losses were replaced by Spanish volunteers. It was a Spaniard, Major Valledor, who led the XVth Brigade. A leader in the 1934 revolt of Asturias, he had recently escaped from imprisonment by the Nationalists and had managed to pull together the Republican forces.

fighters. In group one were Hotto, an ex-captain in the English navy, who had left his submarine to fight with the Republicans; Harrison, a Canadian, a crack pistol shot and our instructor in knife throwing; Léon, a Swiss schoolteacher nicknamed the Tiger, a crack machine-gunner; Van Derart, a Dutchman, skinny but very agile, adventurous, a crack pistol shot and very fast; Jones Vallier, a black American, very nice, expert with a knife. He drove the truck assigned to our platoon.

In group two, my own, was a big Dutchman nick-named Mac. A great fighter, very brave, obedient under orders, ammunition carrier for our small caliber mortar. He was also my liaison agent. Jimmie, a blond Irishman, mortar carrier, handy with a knife. Johnny, an American electrician who took care of the radio. Jean Eureka, the Czech, excellent shot with a machine gun, nick-named the Airplane Shooter. Very small, nervous, he spoke little. Pierre Picard, a Swiss, cook by trade. He knew several countries. He was ammunition carrier.

In group three there was Hirmand, a blond-haired German, member of the German Communist party. He was big, an instructor in the use of all types of arms: pistol, revolver, machine gun, hand grenade. He also gave lessons in laying mines and planting dynamite. He was our explosives man. Verterent, a Belgian from Liège, no known trade, obedient, a man you could count on; handled any weapon, preferably the grenade. He carried the light ammunition. Maccarie, an American, kitchen helper, a good soldier, did all the platoon's work. Tommie Gravaudi, an American, very big but very lazy, always sitting down or sleeping, but who became ex-tremely powerful in action; very handy with a dagger and a good grenade thrower. Hurt Commerkirch, a Pole, big, a good pole vaulter. He knew how to defuse mines and how to study terrain. He was the observer for the platoon, and like me always carried a pair of binoculars. He knew all about traps, ambushes and ruses.

We stayed at the farm almost a month. Each morning we drilled at throwing daggers, taking arms apart and studying mines. Afternoons it was practice at throwing grenades, crossing rivers and climbing rocks in the mountains. We blew up trees and old houses to learn the effects of our explosives. Evenings we were free to go into the town of Olot. There were never any arguments. We were all good friends.

Reconnaissance Operations
on the Ebro

O NE MORNING, the fourteenth of April, we embarked in three Russian Sturka trucks with all our equipment. We drove all day, all night without lights, and all the next morning. We stopped at a little village that had been entirely destroyed by bombing. Not a single inhabitant was left, but the rabbits, chickens, pigs, and goats wandered around freely. The trucks left. We took two mules and a donkey from the village. We loaded them with our supplies and climbed up the mountain. At its summit we found an abandoned convent. We set up our headquarters there. The convent was full of stores: olive oil, sacks of rice, beans, and chick-peas. In the cellars there were good wines and lots of ham. Our two cooks wouldn't have any trouble making good meals, what with all the chickens, rabbits, piglets, lambs, etc. The two mules and the donkey gorged themselves with barley and even tried to eat the sacks.

From the top of our mountain we could watch over the river Ebro. The enemy was on the other side. The front was calm. We were there to observe the movement of troops and the placing of machine guns and artillery. The enemy fired only when we went down to the springs for water. But we weren't unhappy. Every two days we loaded the mules with empty water jugs and a patrol would go to one of the abandoned villages. Along with the water, the patrol would bring back little onions, tomatoes, new potatoes, even radishes, not to mention lettuce and cherries.

In our position we didn't need any trenches; the artillery and bomb craters were our shelter. Things went on like this for three weeks. All was calm. We explored the region. What was surprising was that there were too few of us to hold the front. On patrol we'd have to go five or ten miles to meet one of our units; and when we did they were dug in, amusing themselves or sleeping. They walked in the mountains and even into the villages unarmed, which was rather dangerous.

One evening during supper our lookout reported two enemy soldiers crossing the river. They climbed up on the banks; they were unarmed. We went down to meet them. One was a staff doctor, the other a sergeant who had decided to join the Republicans. I questioned them. They gave us some interesting information; there were plenty of Nationalists facing us, but they had no orders to attack, only to hold us in this area while the army operated in another sector. I notified the general staff of the XVth Brigade. Two days later the prisoners were taken off to Barcelona.

Then the day came that ended our easy life. Each evening we had to cross the river. It was easy; there was little water — it only came to our waists — and the current was weak. On land we took the enemy posts by surprise. Almost always we had to deal with Moroccan Tabors. We knifed sentries, heaved a few grenades, and almost every evening we brought back eight or ten prisoners. They were questioned and then shot, because when the enemy captured one of our men, they took pleasure in cutting off his head and sticking it up on one of their tent poles.

One night we mounted a more important operation with all three groups. This time we were going to surprise the Moroccans right in their own camp. They were very quiet, some playing the flute, others sleeping practically naked. We passed between the sentries, who were walking up and down talking to each other. When we reached the middle of the camp, we started in with the grenades. The sentries were killed on the spot; the others ran off in all directions unarmed. We mowed them down with machine guns, pistols and knives, then finished them off with daggers. It was a real massacre.

Loaded with captured weapons, we left taking four prisoners, Spanish soldiers from Andalucía. The enemy was firing in every direction. But we reached the river and crossed it just in time. A rain of mortar shells fell on the water; machine guns spat bullets. One American got one in his shoulder, but it wasn't a bad wound. I sprained an ankle jumping over a wall. It was very painful but I ran on all the same; it was no time to fall behind. As soon as we crossed the river we hid in our holes and waited. I could see the enemy on the other bank. There were legionnaires,* Moroccans, a few Red Berets,† and Civil Guardsmen. Some of them started to cross the river. But we were ready. Our lookout radioed us a message. Already we were firing nonstop. We slaughtered them; they fell, struggled a moment, then stayed still. I'd downed my twenty-seventh, but I slowed my fire as I was afraid we were running low on ammunition. We fired only at those trying to cross the river.

But our lookout was getting scared. Two hundred yards downstream, an enemy column was starting to cross the river like a flock of sheep. It was the Moroccans. They yelled and waved their rifles in the air. You'd have thought they were dancing. I called together the leaders of the groups to make a decision. They advised that we not retreat but stay hidden in our holes without firing until they'd all crossed the river, then we'd shoot at them in the open. That's what we did. We stopped firing and left on the run. Then we dropped to the ground and crept back through the grass to our holes. But they, thinking we had retreated in disorder, came on across without even keeping low. They crossed

*Members of the Spanish Foreign Legion. V. G.
†Carlists. V. G.

quickly as the water was only up to their ankles; I realized they had opened the dam. They were maybe three or four hundred; strangely, they kept dancing in groups as though at a carnival. Our group three fired the mortar at their rear, very quickly without aiming. The shells fell into the river swarming with men. Then our two machine guns came into action and we fired deliberately, as though at target practice. They fell in heaps. But there were so many they kept on coming. Now there was firing on both sides. Shells whistled over our heads. Two of our men were killed and one was badly wounded. The battle raged. The enemy didn't stop firing. We stuck it out for two hours and twenty-five minutes. The enemy column was stopped in front of us, the survivors hidden behind a wall of corpses. But we were outflanked on both sides. We thought ourselves lost when we heard a clanking noise behind us. We could see two of our Russian tanks coming out of a convent on our right, and behind them a whole company. Just in time. We leapt out of our holes firing a storm of bullets. The tanks reached the river, shooting point-blank. Then they went into the water. What a massacre! The river was red with blood and you could cross it without touching the water, it was so full of corpses. We took a hundred and fifty prisoners and counted around six hundred dead or wounded.

In my platoon we were missing four men; a Swiss and an American killed, and an American and a Belgian evacuated to a hospital with wounds that weren't too bad. I got out of it with the sprained ankle. I came back limping, but I stayed with my "lions." That was the name for them all right.

When we got back to the convent we had to hide in the cellars. Night and day artillery and planes constantly sent us visitors. Everything burned, everything shook. But we weren't afraid; the cellars were solid and well supplied. From reports on our radio I learned that we had uncovered the preparations for an enemy attack. Our strike had shattered it. We had advanced as far as the Nationalists' third position. We'd brought back arms, ammunition, thirty-seven mules and seven Italian cannons. The Republican troops had lost only forty men. Sixty-four wounded stopped at our convent and then were evacuated by hospital train to Barcelona.*

We stayed in shelter three days. Then one morning between bombardments we went down the mountain and got into three trucks. We traveled a day and a night and found ourselves back in Torre de Fontaubella, in the province of Tarragona.

We camped a mile from the village in a hazelnut grove. Around us there were other battalions from the International Brigades; the Garibaldi, the Maptan, the Lincoln, and even a squadron of Polish cavalry. Along the road soldiers drilled. There were sentries everywhere but they didn't stop anyone. We remained there for a rest. We went on training exercises in the mountains to pass the time. We found good things to eat along the paths. Evenings we went into the village to get a couple of jugs of wine; Piavrato, dark and sweet and up to forty-four proof. We passed the evenings under the hazelnut trees. We sat in a circle with the jug of wine in

---

*Following this action, Francisco (who had been a sergeant) was made a lieutenant. V.G.

the middle. The hazelnuts were starting to be good to eat and we picked lots. The bag would be beside the pitcher; we ate and drank steadily. Then we went to sleep on the spot. But we didn't run any risk: the soldiers of the brigades stood guard.

The Franco-Belgians had their camp next to ours. Every morning I went to see them. We spoke French and smoked Gauloises. One evening they invited the whole platoon and we spent the night singing and dancing and drinking. I couldn't take it very long. I went to sleep in a stable by the cows. It was open, there was plenty of air, and it was hot. I felt good.

After two weeks, the trucks came back. They brought reinforcements. I got four men to fill out my outfit, an American, two Poles, and a Finn. We also were given some new material: a special outfit, rubber pants, nylon string, inflatable bags for transporting arms and equipment without getting it wet, all black. The Finn was an excellent swimmer. He taught us all the tricks of swimming quietly, especially underwater and cross-current.

And then we left for an unknown destination.

Raid at the Mouth
of the Ebro

WE CROSSED many mountains. Then the trucks dropped us off near a beach at the mouth of the river Ebro by a steel bridge that had been demolished in the middle.

We hid in a cane field. It wasn't very wide but it stretched a long way along the river. We ate some of our fresh supplies and canned goods, but we could only eat before eleven o'clock. After that nothing, because we had to swim across the river. It was a very hot day. We were thirsty, but the water was fifteen yards away and besides we were forbidden to go up to it.

Our two observers spotted a railroad and a cottage on the other side of the river, but no movement. Behind the railroad was a path on a lower level where enemy soldiers could move without our being able to see them. The front was calm. There were a few shots from time to time. Two Spanish soldiers* stood guard on the bridge.

---

*Francisco always makes a distinction between "soldiers" and Civil Guardsmen, Moroccans, or Italians. The "soldiers" he refers to were Spaniards who had been drafted, not volunteers or mercenaries. V. G.

A little before midnight we undressed and put on our special outfits. The Finn was the first into the water. He had a reel of nylon line on his back with one end secured to our bank. As he advanced, the reel unwound. When he reached the other side, he tied the line to the trunk of a fig tree. Following the line we all crossed, carrying our arms and clothes in the waterproof bags. They didn't see us. Once again on land we hid ourselves in a small hollow under the fig tree. There we took out our outfits: some were to wear legionnaires' costumes; the Dutchman and I Civil Guard uniforms; and two others were dressed as soldiers with wooden buttons. This took us about an hour's time.

When we were dressed and had our weapons ready we crossed the railroad and went down the road. Not a soul was in sight. Coming up behind the cottage we found a lighted window. We surrounded the house, but first I sent two men to take care of the two sentries on the bridge.

Inside they were playing the accordion, laughing and singing. I jerked open the door and saw a major, two captains and some dozen soldiers, unarmed and half drunk, some without shoes and in shirtsleeves, sitting on unmade beds. They knew right away what was happening. They gave themselves up, hands held high, except for the major, who threw a stool. The little Czech hit him with a burst of his tommy gun. After that it was quiet. We made them go out. The two sentries had been taken by surprise and killed. We pushed our prisoners onto the bridge. In the middle there was a wooden passway where you had to go carefully, one at a time. Once the prisoners were handed over to group three, who'd stayed on the bank, we went back to the cottage where group one awaited us. We got under way, crossing a hill full of big holes in the side of the rock. We followed a path, advancing haltingly, and fell into a hole full of sleeping soldiers, Carlists dressed as legionnaires but wearing their red berets. The Dutchman and I, in Civil Guard uniforms, went forward. A soldier got up and asked us if we'd like a place to sleep. At the bottom of the hole there was a green Italian cannon. I grasped the situation. I went out and looked around me: I counted four big holes. Quickly I put three men in front of each hole at a distance of about twenty yards. At the signal they all threw grenades into the holes. The enemy came out like rats. Then we blew up the munitions, not taking any prisoners but rather letting them run unarmed into the mountains.

On the way back we stopped a supply truck. We set fire to it after killing the occupants, two Italians that we recognized by their plumed hats.

Then I lit a green flare to indicate the end of the operations. We dressed and swam back across the river. Suddenly there was a burst of machine-gun fire. An Englishman was killed. But one of our observers, who was stationed on the enemy bank with three comrades to cover us, located the gunner's position. They took him from behind and made him prisoner. They took his machine gun and swam across the river with it, making him swim in front. I met him at the other bank. I spoke to him in Spanish; he answered in Italian. So we killed him.

Cost of the operation: the Englishman killed, a Pole wounded in the left leg. On the enemy side: a major, two captains, seven Carlists and three Italians killed, and eleven Spanish prisoners. Booty: one machine gun and twenty-eight grenades. Destroyed: four Italian cannons.

All morning there was a hurly-burly on the enemy side of the river. They fired and fired with their cannons, mortars and automatic weapons. Around ten o'clock some fighter planes appeared in the sky. It seemed they'd spotted our refuge. They strafed our cane field from all directions. By luck, no one was hit, though the bullets whistled around our heads. But the little Czech had put his machine gun into position. Just as one of the planes dove over us, he fired up at it in the pattern of a cross. The pilot was hit and the plane fell into the river. From the other bank, the Fascists tried to cover him with their fire. But the plane had fallen near our bank. With our binoculars the observer and I watched the plane sink, and no one got out. Later, a diver from my group went into the water to check. The pilot had died in the cockpit.

In the afternoon we left the cane field in single file. Republican soldiers, a lot of them, had come to relieve us. We got into the trucks. They took us to Barcelona, where we were given leave.

Leave in Barcelona

W E GOT OFF at the Karl Marx Barracks, near the
zoo. We were so hungry we went straight to the
kitchen. We ate as much as we liked and drank gallons
of wine. Our time was our own; there was no guard
duty. We got a pack of cigarettes a day. We got our pay
and bonuses. I received fifty thousand pesetas for each
of the men.

We wandered around the town, especially the Barrio
Chino. We went to the movies, made friends. I went to
visit the Pole at the Calle Tallere hospital. He was in a
single room and was being well cared for.

We spent two weeks like this. Then we reconstituted
my group of sixteen men, the same ones plus two newcomers. For once there were comrades who spoke Spanish. One was a Mexican lieutenant about fifty years old
with a big belly, tatooed all over and covered with scars
from fights. The other was a chocolate-colored Cuban
lieutenant. He was always drinking, always smiling; a
good man with a knife.

There was nothing to be surprised at in the presence
of officers in my group; they were just comrades like the
rest. We were under a special rule in our units. Men

were picked for their abilities. I remained the leader of my unit. It was I who received orders from the general staff, always at the last minute. Then I gave the orders for their execution.

One morning it was time to go. We left in two trucks. In the evening we got off in a little village near Falset. We camped under some hazelnut trees at the edge of a ravine between two hills.

Mornings we went to one hill or the other to practice shooting at cans. Afternoons we shot at rabbits. There were thousands of them. We had fun killing them and then eating them. We gave lots of them to the villagers. In exchange they gave us fish, onions, tomatoes, cherries, hazelnuts, and of course wine.

We lived like this a good while. In wartime you live from day to day; you don't bother with the calendar. I realized when the Fourteenth of July came because of the festival in the village. A battalion put on a parade. The square was filled with tables and benches and we were invited to a big feast. I saw Commissar Tito, the Yugoslav. I'd known him in Barcelona.* We talked to-

*Francisco had met Tito at the general headquarters of the International Brigade, the Karl Marx Barracks in Barcelona. Tito (whose real name was Josip Broz), was the leader of the Communist party in Yugoslavia and had organized an underground railway, starting in Paris, to transport volunteers from Eastern Europe to Spain. From 1946 to 1950 Stalin held in suspicion all Eastern European Communists who had fought in Spain; and Tito himself denied having been in Spain. "But," says Hugh Thomas (*The Spanish Civil War*, p. 298), "it seems probable that he at least visited the Brigades' headquarters for one reason or another." Francisco's testimony confirms this historical point. Tito, as political commissioner of the XVth Brigade, visited Francisco just before the latter set off to join in the battle of the Ebro. V. G.

gether and he invited my whole platoon to his table. We lived it up, drank it up. There were as many cigars and cigarettes as you wanted. Then busses arrived from Barcelona. Girls wearing soldiers' uniforms got out. They joined us, and we started all over again, eating and drinking with them. By evening I and a few others from my platoon were crocked. Our comrades brought us back to camp and I slept all night and part of the next day, guarded by my faithful friend and orderly the Dutchman so that I wouldn't do anything stupid. But in the country hangovers go away fast. When I woke up I took a good shower. The Cuban and the Mexican waited for me to go back to the village, they to continue celebrating, I to go get orders.

The next day the disinfection truck arrived at the camp. We all went through. That felt good. They gave us clean clothes and sent our dirty ones to the laundry. That wasn't so good, as it always happened on the eve of an attack. It didn't fool us. I received the orders: we were to prepare our weapons and outfits and wait for the trucks. The next day they arrived and we left for an unknown destination.

The Battle of the Ebro

The Republican general staff had decided upon offensive action — with the aim of crossing the Ebro at a number of crucial locations, in order to disrupt the communications network of the Nationalist forces and (if possible) to reestablish contact between Cataluña and the province of Valencia, which had been cut off since the beginning of April by the Nationalist army. After the Aragón offensive, their only access to the sea had been through Vinaroz and Castellón de la Plana.

The Republicans had put together a whole new army for this audacious attempt: the "Army of the Ebro" under the leadership of General Modesto. The Army of the Ebro included the XVth Army Corps under Tagüena and the Vth Army Corps under Lister; and in reserve, the XVIIIth Army Corps. Altogether about one hundred thousand men. This army was to confront the Moroccan army under the command of General Yagüe.

The battle of the Ebro was destined to pass through the same phases as those of Brunete and Teruel: first a successful attack, then a holding action achieved by Nationalist reinforcements, then a counterattack. The consequences of the counterattack were disastrous for the Republican side. The battle of the Ebro was the last major battle of the Spanish war.

In the night of 24 July, under a moonless sky, the crossing of the river began. The chief of staff of the XVth International Brigade, an Englishman named

65

Malcolm Dunbar, had selected the locations for the crossing: doubtless on the basis of the reconnaissance operations carried out by the commandos, including Francisco's unit. The XVth Brigade was to cross the river between Flix and Mora, at the spot reconnoitered by Francisco and his troop in April and May. Still farther south, the XIVth Brigade (French and Belgian) crossed the river near its mouth at Amposta.

Francisco's unit crossed south of Mora, towards Miravet. Working to the enemy's rear (Francisco encountered a second time the Moroccan forces under Yagüe) that unit seems to have had for its mission cutting off the main road from Zaragoza, which ran between Gandesa and Corbera about 9 miles beyond the river.

V. G.

DURING THE NIGHT we descended into the countryside. We advanced along a road that followed the river Ebro. We'd taken our special river-crossing outfits. The Finn was happy as could be; his turn had come again. We posted ourselves at a certain point beside the river and waited orders. At one in the morning we got the order to cross.

The Finn was the first in the water, with his reel of nylon line on his back. Once on the enemy bank, he took out the cables we'd prepared and tied them to a tree. They would be used to guide the boats that were to transport our troops and their weapons. When our group reached the enemy bank, we silently took off our swimming outfits and put on Nationalist uniforms which we'd brought over in the waterproof bags. We regrouped in the underbrush on the riverbank while the rest of our troops started crossing the river in the boats, following the cables we'd stretched.

Leaving the troops to take their positions, we set off guerrilla fashion, marching ten yards apart in single file. After two or three miles we reached the main road to Madrid. There, near a little bridge, we prepared an ambush in some pits with our machine guns and light mortars in firing position. The order was to fire without question on all vehicles that passed. We couldn't make a mistake; the troops that landed after us had gone northwards by way of Asco and Flix. We were facing south towards Corbera and Gandesa. We were there to block the route off to the enemy, who after our attack would attempt to seek refuge at Corbera and beyond. We were about seven miles behind the front at the Ebro.

A soldier coming from Corbera appeared at the beginning of the bridge. He carried a suitcase. We stopped him. Since we wore Nationalist uniforms he didn't worry. He was an Aragonese soldier coming from Zaragoza, where he'd been on leave. He informed us about his company. He was very young. I signed his pass and ordered him to go to Falset, a town nine miles across the river on the Republican side.

Near the bridge there was a large house. All of a sudden one of the windows lit up. I dispatched a patrol of four men. They came back with seven prisoners, all Civil Guardsmen. So as not to make any noise we killed them with our daggers. We stripped them and threw the corpses into the pit, and seven of us changed our Nationalist uniforms for those of Civil Guardsmen. The uniform I got was a marvel; it fit as though made to my measurements. Then we stood guard on the bridge while the others hid in the pits, ready to fire.

A truck came up. We stopped it. It was full of people, civilians and military. We questioned the civilians and released them. The soldiers we took prisoner, except for two Civil Guardsmen that we killed immediately.

Now bunches of enemy soldiers came running from the direction of Mora and Asco to get away from our men. We kept on stopping them. They had thrown away their weapons. Many got away into the countryside. We couldn't stop everybody, so I gave the order to let everyone pass except for officers, Civil Guardsmen, and Moroccans. Those we killed.*

Then our troops arrived. We were ordered to set up an ambush at the entrance to Corbera. Right away we loaded our equipment onto the truck we had captured from the enemy. When we came in sight of the town we got off and made the same maneuver; those in Civil Guard uniforms stood guard on the road, the rest hid in pits, and again we let some pass and shot others. After several hours our troops arrived, tired from running after the enemy, who had retreated in disorder. Now the squadron of Polish cavalry joined us and cleaned up the countryside as far as the foot of the mountains. Only a few isolated snipers returned our fire.

---

*"At half-past two in the morning, a message from Colonel Peñarredonda (in command of the sector of Mora [where Francisco's unit was operating]) reached Yagüe. The Republicans had crossed the Ebro, some of Peñarredonda's units had heard firing from behind, and he and his divisional headquarters had lost contact with their flanks. This Colonel was one of the most unpleasant and inefficient in the Nationalist army. He had a particular hatred of the International Brigades and, on his own responsibility, gave orders that any of them captured should be shot" (Thomas, *The Spanish Civil War*, p. 545). This was the reason for Francisco's attitude towards the prisoners. V. G.

But our advance had been too rapid: there were no troops to the rear, so those who were on the line, like us, had to wait for dawn to receive orders. At daybreak a motorcycle courier brought us the order to take the town of Corbera. We attacked at once. In the main street we advanced in two lines close to the sidewalks. The other companies surrounded the town. When we were halfway down the main street we were fired on from a bakery on a corner. Two of my men were killed. The group behind us covered us with their fire while we attacked the bakery with grenades. Then it was quiet. We went in. It was a woman who had fired at us. She was lying there dead, riddled with grenade fragments, still holding her machine gun in her arms. We searched the building. In the cellar, hidden behind some sacks, we found three German pilots. One of them fired at the Belgian, who was wounded in the right thigh. We immediately shot the three Germans where they stood.

The column resumed its advance. Bullets whistled at the edge of town. I had to make the men hide in doorways. We waited for something to happen for an interminable half hour. Then we advanced by spurts, guerrilla style, using each hole, each obstacle, shooting at anything that moved. Suddenly four legionnaires appeared on the street firing at us. We let them advance; at twenty yards we shot them almost point-blank.

We continued along the street. We came to a cemetery. It was encircled by a wall a yard high. We took shelter behind the wall and counted heads. Of my sixteen men, eleven were left. Three had been killed, one was wounded, one was missing. The town had been taken. We awaited new orders. An hour later the order came to take the cemetery. Apparently it was full of enemy soldiers, hiding even in the tombs. That explained the noises we'd heard behind the wall as though someone had been smashing rocks; they'd been opening the tombs to hide in them. Our two observers had spotted a big gathering of the enemy in the middle of the cemetery. With my eleven men, we were not very strong. But our other men were late coming. We had to decide what to do.

The Czech and the Mexican followed the wall and discovered a breach. The Czech mounted his machine gun in it and the Mexican loaded the mortar. He would shell the gate to get the ones coming out. The rest of us would leap over the wall and advance, avoiding the tombs.

At two in the afternoon our English observer in a treetop spied a whole crowd of the enemy entering the cemetery gate. We jumped the wall. What a cracking! They fired at us from all sides. We had to fight man to man first with grenades then with knives to clean out each tomb, each one a little fort. Everything exploded out of the tombs, the dead and the living alike. It smelled terrible. None of the enemy wanted to give themselves up. They preferred to die on the spot in the tombs. My platoon was sensational. To recognize each other in the smoke we sang the *"Internationale"* and yelled the password. We advanced slowly. I shouted to the machine gunner and mortarer to cease firing. Then the enemy all came out of their holes to escape by the gate. But we too had gotten into the open tombs and from their shelter we reopened fire. And the enemy went back to his holes. This went on for two hours, when all of a sudden I saw the Mexican leap over the wall followed by a hundred Republican soldiers. So I brought my men out. Surprise — I'd lost four men and I had two wounded, one in the arm, the other on the head. We were only five. So I retreated to the shelter of the wall while our troops cleaned up the cemetery. I cared for the two wounded and then went to the staff to give my report. The major had established his post at the side of the road. Right away he gave me munitions and ten new men; two Danes, a Finn, and seven Poles, cavalrymen who had lost their horses. Since ten that morning enemy aircraft had constantly bombed our rear and the fighter planes had strafed us and launched grenades. Sometimes they hit their own troops as they ran in all directions.

My platoon regrouped, I received the order to advance guerrilla style towards Gandesa, a town three and a half miles from Corbera. We advanced prudently. We found a Republican soldier who had lost his company. I took him on and gave him a rifle, two grenades and a hundred bullets. He followed me like my shadow.

We advanced along the road without finding anything. Next to a wooden cabin I saw an apple tree with fallen apples under it. I went over to pick some up. As I bent over, there was a shot. A bullet went through my cap. The Aragonese, the new soldier who didn't leave my heels, saw the flash. He threw a grenade into the cabin. Inside we found a Civil Guardsman, badly wounded, pistol still in hand. He was well armed. Beside him we found a box of grenades, two machine guns with their ammunition, two boxes of canned goods, and lucky for us, a big box full of cigars, cigarettes, and matches in bulk. We loaded up until we couldn't carry any more, then we threw a grenade and this time everything exploded and caught fire.

We continued to advance. From time to time I sent my courier ahead. Soon we arrived in sight of Gandesa. Leaving the road we moved along the side of a small mountain. We found a big farm. No one was left; the doors and windows were wide open. We searched everywhere; there literally wasn't a soul, but in the stables we found mules, two horses, goats, some cows and even rabbits in cages. The fire was still lit in the house and there was food on the table. We took it and went and hid in a clearing behind the house. We ate. Night came and I decided we would sleep in the straw in the barn. We spent a good night. At dawn the observer on watch in a pine tree saw a column of enemy soldiers coming along the path. They advanced toward the farm like ants. Behind them there was another column with mules carrying machine guns and mortars. We were only about two miles from Gandesa, which it seemed had been taken by our troops at nightfall.* I didn't have enough men to attack the column. So I would try to stop them. We quickly climbed up the mountain. We positioned our two machine guns and I sent two of the Poles to the rear for reinforcements.

The enemy advanced without taking cover as if they were sure of themselves. Through the binoculars I saw them enter the farm. They chased away the cows and

---

*In fact, the Republicans had been unable to take the town, in spite of fierce fighting during which the XVth International Brigade distinguished itself, particularly the English battalion, which took heavy losses. V. G.

took the horses and mules. I saw the leaders giving orders. Then the column was on the march again, advancing in our direction.

From the top of a rock our observer spied another column coming up on our left. This one was made up of Carlists with red berets. They advanced, their white flag at the head. There were not very many of them. They disappeared from my sight as they got under cover of the trees. I was beginning to be worried by the situation. Fortunately, just as I was about to order a retreat one of the Poles arrived, out of breath. Three companies of Lister's corps with mules carrying heavy machine guns were already on their way to join us. But the enemy was advancing on us. I became hopeful though when I saw the soldiers walking like sheep, their rifles slung over their shoulders. There were at least ten enemy scouts inspecting the terrain but they made the mistake of sticking too close to the column.

Enemy reconnaissance planes wheeled above us. Then came the fighter planes, five or six in a line. Well hidden in the brush, in holes or behind rocks, we didn't move an inch. The scouts were only a few yards from us, the column not even fifty. We were going to use the "Indian tactic": let the enemy come almost to us then surprise them. Defense for them was impossible because they had advanced for at least five hundred yards in the open along a rock so steep and slippery that many slipped as they climbed. The scouts were almost at our gunpoints when we shot them. Our machine gun opened fire on the column and we charged, throwing grenades and yelling. The enemy fell like flies, tumbling down the length of the rock. On the left the

Carlist column had come out of the forest. They charged us guerrilla style — but in a thick column. Fortunately our reinforcements had already taken up position. They opened fire. But the enemy still advanced stubbornly even though men were falling constantly.

Behind the column appeared a line of small Italian tanks. Luckily four of our antitank cannons were already in position. But until now neither our cannons nor heavy machine guns had opened fire, so as better to surprise the enemy. With the binoculars I saw the farm full of soldiers. Right away I had the mortarers fire at it. They ran for cover in the forest. The combat had lasted at least thirty minutes when the enemy artillery got into the action. As soon as a shell exploded on our position we ran and got into its crater, for it is rare that two shells will hit the same place. It was very hot, we didn't have any more water and the enemy planes bombed and strafed us. The troops sent by Lister, though hard pressed by the airplane fire, were holding their position and had started digging trenches.

On my side, we'd found a boulder with a crevice at the back. The Finn and the Norwegian and I put a Maxim gun in position there. Two Poles passed the ammunition. The enemy artillery kept raining shells on us. Seven little tanks advanced towards us. Behind them marched legionnaires, Moroccans and some Red Berets. We let them approach to almost point-blank range, then suddenly our cannons, machine guns, grenade launchers, and mortars went into action. Three tanks were stopped; the others turned back. But the enemy re-formed and charged again: a deluge! They were almost on us when another battalion of Republican reinforcements arrived. They relieved my platoon and we withdrew. We were only seven now.

We were supposed to rejoin the general staff of our brigade. We marched part of the night. We were exhausted. We stopped to camp in a field of fig trees. We stayed there three days eating, drinking, smoking, and sleeping, while a short way off the battle continued night and day.

The fig grove was at the foot of a steep hill covered with pines. Below was a road; beside it stood a little house with a vegetable garden. I saw some tomatoes that looked good. I went down to the garden. As I picked a couple of tomatoes I heard a noise. I ducked down in my row of tomatoes. The enemy must have seen me! They fired over me with a machine gun. The bullets went by right above my head. I stretched out flat. But my comrades had heard the shooting and were already there surrounding the house guerrilla style. They attacked it with the grenades and set fire to it with two antitank bombs. The enemy machine-gun fire stopped. Four legionnaires, a Civil Guardsman, and two Red Berets came out through the windows and rear door. We shot them down. One of our Poles got up and went forward to take the Civil Guardsman's weapon. But he was only wounded, playing dead. He fired four shots into the belly of the Pole, who was killed instantly: we returned the fire too late. We abandoned our comrade's body and went back to our fig trees.

Meanwhile the Czech hadn't been wasting his time. He had climbed to the top of a tall pine at the top of the hill and installed his machine gun and a supply of drums. It was a Russian gun. Junker bombers had been flying over in formation all morning, bombing and strafing all around.

We dug a shelter in the roots of a fig tree beside an enormous boulder. In the afternoon, from our hole we counted eleven bombers coming at us, almost touching the trees on the hill. The Czech fired at them like a wild man. One plane caught fire and fell in a spiral. The rest came back and dropped bombs on our hill and the pines caught fire. Other bombers came in four waves; six, six more, then ten, then six more. They pounded the hill. A bomb fell fifteen yards from our hole. The shock broke the trunk of the fig tree. Then it was over. I sent two men to look for the Czech or what was left of him. Surprise! They found him still perched in his tree. All around everything was demolished and burned: only his pine had been spared. He came down from his roost, still panting. He drank a little; he was covered with dirt and his head was full of lumps from flying branches that had hit him. He was happy as a lark to have shot down two planes.

Near the end of the afternoon, a liaison officer from the general staff joined us with nine reinforcements, well armed and loaded with supplies. Then a motorcyclist came with orders: at daybreak we were to leave for the Sierra de Pandols, which had been retaken by the enemy during the last fighting. On our way we were to collect all the strayed soldiers; then, in order to prepare for our counterattack the following morning at daybreak, we were to make a reconnaissance of the enemy positions entrenched at the summit of the sierra.

The nine reinforcements were tired from their march. They came from the Garibaldi Battalion; there were five

Italians and four Frenchmen. Of my men there remained a Cuban, a Mexican, a Czech, an Englishman, a Dutchman, an Irishman; and with myself, a Spaniard, that put us back at sixteen men. Quickly we made friends; we divided up our food and cigarettes, ate, and then slept. At dawn we took to the road. The day would be hot, so we took a lot of water and I ordered the men to drink as little as possible during the march. We advanced slowly, resting frequently. The reinforcements had recovered well, but it was important to arrive at the combat zone well rested. In the distance, artillery and aircraft continued the bombardment. A while later we picked up a soldier, a young Catalan. He was lost but he still had a rucksack full of grenades. He was very frightened. I reassured him and told him to come with me. He was never more than a foot away, like a little dog. Farther on we passed a battalion going to the front. Then we entered a gorge full of caves. They were occupied by doctors and nurses caring for the wounded laid out on stretchers. There were other caves piled with the dead. Ambulances continually brought in more wounded by the dozens. We passed by a cave where a kitchen had been set up. They gave us hot broth and a large loaf of bread each. The gorge widened to a breadth of three or four hundred yards; there were more caves full of resting or slightly wounded soldiers. We went along like this for quite a while, marching single file. When we came to the end of the gorge we saw the Sierra de Pandols. We were separated from it by a field about a hundred and fifty yards across. We saw corpses everywhere. Beyond it was the sierra, like a big rock wall, covered with trees shattered by the bombardments. On top, we could see the trenches from which the enemy fired at anything that moved. I gave the order to advance in starts, keeping well separated, guerrilla style. If anyone was wounded, he must crawl forward, never backward. We crossed without trouble, taking a few rounds of mortar fire. At the foot of the sierra we were protected by the steep rocks. On the right, I saw at least two companies ready for the attack. A little higher there was another, its men hidden in the rocks. There were heaps of corpses and they smelled. The enemy fired continually on the reinforcements crossing the field to join the troops ready for the attack. To obey orders, I now had to lead my platoon as close as possible to the crest of the sierra so we could observe the enemy carefully. I decided to ascend on the left side of the mountain. Progressing from rock to rock, we got halfway up the slope and hid behind a wall of rocks. The Mexican got on my nerves a little; he kept joking with the Cuban. The young Catalan shook like a leaf; he stayed glued to me, shooting frightened glances everywhere.

We had to wait for the night to get any closer to the enemy. The sun was strong and our supply of water was almost exhausted. By chance I noticed a little spring of bubbling water fifty yards below us. But it was under enemy fire: there were already four corpses around it. I asked for a volunteer; the Irishman left with the canteens. He went down little by little; not a shot was fired. Hidden behind a corpse, he filled the canteens, put them on his shoulder, and came back up. He hadn't gone twenty yards when the enemy, who had watched him, let loose. He fell, crawled a couple yards, then stayed still, in the shelter of a rock. Would he move again? No, he'd been killed. So I sprang out and went down, moving in quick dashes. I reached the Irishman. He was dead all right. Hidden by the rock I picked up the canteens. Only two had been hit. Then I came back up, jumping from rock to rock. The enemy played with me, shooting in bursts with a machine gun. Well, I would have some fun with them too! I took a rock and put it in my cap. I threw it to the right; the shots rang out and I went to the left. I was in the shelter of a clump of shrubs with twenty yards of uncovered ground still to go. I rested a good minute. I saw my friends getting worried; they must be thinking I was dead. I saw the Mexican getting ready to come down. So I sprang out and ran like a madman with my canteens. Twenty yards can sometimes seem like a long way. Bullets grazed me, but I arrived safe and sound in an explosion of joy. We divided the water. There were three full canteens left. I gave them to the Dutchman to watch.

Now we had to wait for night. The hours passed slowly. Then we saw some Republican tanks appear on the plain. Their cannons fired at the enemy trenches and the battalion highest up attacked. Then came a deluge of shells and bullets. Grenades thrown from the heights tumbled down the mountain. Our men were mowed down. Some got to within a hundred yards of the summit but were nailed. This went on for thirty minutes. Then everything stopped except that the enemy fired on anything that moved: the wounded and those who went to get them.

My observer had gone out on reconnaissance towards the left. He came back to get me. Crawling, we reached the clump of shrubs where he'd made a little hole. This was a surprise! From here you had a view of the enemy trenches. First was a machine-gun nest, then ten yards farther the entrance to the trenches, and beyond that the whole line. The trenches were swarming like an anthill. I noticed that the soldiers arrived from the left, behind the machine-gun nest. I also spotted the start of a path that had to go down on the other side.

Two hours later our men attacked again. But it couldn't have worked; attacking from the front meant only a useless massacre. Three soldiers from that attack had taken refuge in a rock below us. I signaled to them and they joined us. They were Andalusians. We gave them a little water and right away one of them started sounding off; he called us cowards because we were so close to the enemy and still didn't attack. I explained our purpose and the orders we had received. Then he calmed down. The two others in turn explained what they were doing; and they said that that night they were supposed to attack with grenades. I told them that if I could see their leader I could help him a great deal in taking the position. I took the angry one to the observation post and gave him the binoculars. He looked, but not for long. "I'll go see the major; he's at the base of the hill with three companies of volunteers."

An hour later I saw the Andalusian moving up the mountain in short dashes followed by four officers. In passing, the Andalusian collected the dead men's rucksacks. They all arrived without trouble; a major, a captain, and two lieutenants. I showed them my orders, then took them to the observation post. Still the same hurly-burly in the enemy camp: some coming in through the connecting trench, others leaving by the path with the wounded. Moroccans appeared with their white pants and brown burnooses, rifles slung over their shoulders. After a good look, the major said he'd change his plans; one company would attack from the front, following the general staff's orders, but the two others would attack from my side. I agreed but asked that the two companies not make their move before my attack. If it succeeded I would light two flares, red and green, to signal our position, and then the other companies could join us. The major and his officers were very pleased and left me the three Andalusians.

The enemy was continually on the alert. They fired at anything that moved and threw grenades at the wounded stretched out behind the rocks. Finally night came. The coolness was soothing as we were all feverish from heat and thirst. The poor Irishman hadn't died for nothing; without water we couldn't have held out, and we had to be in shape for what we were going to do. Now everything seemed calm. The moonlight was beautiful. Above us they were working on the trenches. We heard the sounds of pickaxes and spades. A Moroccan sang as he pushed a wheelbarrow; when he came to the entrance of the connecting trench he emptied it over the edge. The rocks tumbled down the slope, passing over our heads. The hours passed. Then our artillery started firing. Some way off to the right we picked out the battalion mounting the attack. The enemy started firing. Our moment had come. I gave my orders in a lowered voice; I would go ahead with my men; the newcomers from the Garibaldi Battalion, whom I'd never seen in combat, would follow behind. The Andalusians would advance on my right. My little Catalan was to follow close enough to touch me, carrying supplies and grenades. Above all, no talking and take care not to set a single stone rolling. We started crawling in the direction of the machine gun; then we veered a bit to the left and stopped in a fold of terrain that hid us well. We were less than ten yards from the entrance to the connecting trench. We heard men speaking and once in a while the Moroccan would return with his wheelbarrow and empty it on our heads. I prepared the red flare for the Dutchman to light when we launched our surprise attack. I waited a little impatiently. It seemed to me our men were late in advancing. It was true that it was hard to advance upward toward a trench from which the enemy could make it rain grenades. That's what I was waiting for. When the grenades burst it would mean our men had come into range; just behind us the two companies should be ready to pounce.

All of a sudden there was the noise of grenades with machine-gun fire on the right. We sprang forward throwing our grenades. The machine gun was taken by surprise, its four gunners killed. The Czech was already in the connecting trench and his machine gun sprayed the length of the trench mowing down everything. The others advanced on both sides throwing grenades. The Dutchman lit the red flare and then took up his post at the head of the path and mowed down everyone who came up or tried to escape. Soon there were no men left in the trench; they had abandoned their weapons and run off in all directions. I shot the green flare about two hundred yards from the entrance to the connecting trench where the red one had burned and the three companies hurried to join us. I told my Andalusians to call for twenty Spanish volunteers as it seemed that my men had taken losses. Then I set off, the little Catalan still on my heels. On my left our men went down the trail. I chose the right. I searched the enemy batteries. I counted my men: nine were missing. But the Andalusians had turned out to be experienced soldiers; I could count on them. The ground dropped quickly. I had to stop frequently to look around to make sure I wasn't suddenly surrounded. The Moroccans and legionnaires knew how to let you pass in order to kill you from behind. When they were captured they often told us they were more Red than Negrín: they were traitors, and disarmed traitors are cowards. But when they're ahead they fight dirty, and as we came down I lost two men and had one badly wounded from that trick of theirs.

Two of the major's companies descended the trail on my left; the third held the position at the sierra's summit. When I got to the bottom the Sierra de Caballs was on my right. We went rapidly around it and from behind captured by surprise twenty-one Italian cannons, seventeen trucks loaded with shells, and thirty-two Italians, whom I handed over to one of the major's companies as we were now going to climb up the back of the Sierra de Caballs. We took it without fighting. The enemy had fled from the top leaving all the equipment and guns in position. The 1st Company of El Campesino* joined us. They were well armed. A captain consulted with me and we set off in the direction of La

_____
El Campesino (The Peasant) was a very well-known and popular guerrilla leader who had become a division commander. V. G.

Viuda. It was now full daylight. We were very tired from covering many miles climbing up and down on the run. But when you've won a victory you can't let it go. We took La Viuda after brief fighting. The enemy quickly raised their arms. They were Carlists. Surrendering was unusual for them; usually they fought to the death. In this last combat I had losses again: more than half my attack force (including those who had joined us). Fortunately the wounded were quickly taken away by the stretcher bearers of the International Brigade. The ambulances were already at the foot of the mountain. The enemy was silent; once in a while there was a cannon or mortar shot. Our spirits rose again.

Now I counted my own men: I still had those two devils the Cuban and the Mexican; my courier the Dutchman; the Englishman, Captain Hotto; the Finn, although he was wounded in the shoulder; and the Czech, who had been waddling like a duck since coming down from his pine tree. There were also two Frenchmen, an Italian, and my faithful dog the Catalan. We were eleven, having lost six comrades.

My mission was accomplished. I now had to return to the International Brigade general staff for orders as I was responsible to them and no one else. After a little rest, we went back the way we had come. But we had to watch for enemy snipers looking for a kill. We had received food and tobacco and had filled our canteens at the river. We moved along quietly. When we came to a wood that had been spared by the shells we rested in its shelter, as we had to stay out of sight of planes. We found ourselves back in the plain at the foot of the Sierra de Pandols. It was still a dangerous area, still under mortar fire. We went bit by bit, guerrilla style, and entered the gorge. Then I realized I'd lost my little Catalan. Had he been wounded? I went back, but I couldn't see anyone on the plain. I came back to the gorge. There we advanced with difficulty. It was full of corpses and wounded men in agony. The enemy had located the gorge and shelled it. Shells fell in front of us, then behind; the caves were crammed with soldiers waiting for the end of the bombardment. The planes, too, had spotted the gorge; they machine-gunned it from one end to another. We kept having to dive for cover. There was so much strafing I gave the order to find shelter. We entered a cave that was already half full. More soldiers came in and we were packed in like anchovies in a barrel. To my surprise, I found my little Catalan there. He had lost us and gone ahead thinking he'd catch up with us again. The time I had wasted in looking for him was going to cost us dearly. The mortar fire came closer. All of a sudden several shells exploded in the mouth of the cave. We were thrown on top of each other. Then the firing grew distant; the wave was over. I'd gotten a fragment in my right thigh. I got up to leave the cave and fell at the first step. The Dutchman looked at the wound. He tore off a sleeve of his shirt and made a tight dressing. The little Catalan got several fragments in the head and died instantly. The English captain was wounded in the arm and slightly in the side. The Italian and one Frenchman were killed. The cave rang with the screams of the wounded.

We were only nine now, including four wounded. My

wound didn't look too bad. But I couldn't even get up; my leg was paralyzed. The five men still unhurt had a hard time getting us out. But we were lucky; two stretcher bearers of the XVth Brigade arrived, each with a stretcher. They laid the Englishman and me on them. The comrades didn't leave us; they took turns carrying us. We came to a clearing by the river. An ambulance was hidden in a cane field under a camouflage of canes. Doctors and nurses cared ceaselessly for the wounded. Just as our two stretchers were put down some planes came over and made four passes, strafing and dropping grenades. Slaughter. The Cuban got the full force of one grenade. He was in pieces. That hurt me very much; he was a brave soldier. Captain Hotto was wounded in both legs while lying on the stretcher. The Finn was still standing, but his right ear was half torn off. We were only eight now.

A captain came along who recognized me. Right away he had my stretcher and the Englishman's loaded into a four-place ambulance that had just pulled up. The Finn, an Andalusian soldier and the Dutchman climbed in and sat between the stretchers. The Czech, who still had his machine gun, got in back and the Frenchman got in with the driver, a huge black American wearing a helmet. We started — slowly, as the road was full of holes and ruts and the bumps made the stretchers bounce. I didn't suffer too much, but the Englishman groaned with pain. Then we came to a road and went faster. But in places the road was cut by bomb craters. The able men had to get out and push the ambulance on a detour through the fields. We came to a village. We stopped and they gave each of us a bowl of milk, some biscuits and a cigarette. We got back on the road, but a few miles farther on we were attacked by planes. Our driver zigzagged while our comrades held us on our stretchers. Then the driver turned into a little woods and all those who were able jumped out and hid under the trees.

The Czech didn't leave me. He just took his machine gun and sat on the back of the ambulance. Three planes circled above us. From where I was I could see them pass just above the treetops. The planes banked in turning and you got a good view of the pilots. Two planes flew over spitting bullets. The Czech fired at the third just as it turned. I had a good view of the pilot getting hit in the head. A moment later we heard the explosion of the plane as it fell beyond the trees. The two others came back on the attack, but this time they made their turns out of range. Then we saw them dive towards us. The Czech didn't move from my side. The moment the first plane opened fire the Czech replied, firing constantly. When the second came, the Czech had finished his drum and didn't have another. So he lay on top of me. The burst shook the ambulance. When the Czech got up, we saw that the burst had hit the Englishman and the Finn, who were lying across from me. They were dead, riddled with bullets. There was a moment of silence, then we heard the shouts and calls of our comrades. The Dutchman ran up. He thought we were dead. He said the second plane had landed not far away, near the road. He took off again. A few minutes later he was back with some soldiers carrying the wounded pilot. They took the Englishman's corpse from the stretcher and put the German pilot on it. He wore a green uniform. He spoke in German with the Czech. On the first pass he had gotten a bullet in the arm and another in the leg. At the second pass his gas tank had been hit. He had known he couldn't make it back to his base so he had come down.

The Frenchman had been killed. We put his body on top of the other two and left again. The German pilot had closed his eyes; he didn't say anything more. A little later we realized he was dead. He must have bled to death. We reached the bank of the Ebro at nightfall. We took out the dead. They were buried in a big hole dug on the riverbank. Each ambulance that came sorted out the dead and the living and left its corpses in the hole. After an hour my stretcher was put into a boat. The Czech, who still had his machine gun, the Dutchman, the fat Mexican and four other wounded crossed the river with me. On the other bank they carried me five hundred yards and we all hid in a cane field. Another hour passed and an ambulance came to pick us up.

I was put on a hospital train marked all over with red crosses. They applied a new dressing and put me on the upper stretcher. The Czech, whose foot was all swollen, was put below me. The Dutchman and the Mexican got into the trucks.

The train rolled gently. We stopped frequently. From time to time they brought us milk and cigarettes. I gave mine to the Czech. He smoked standing up, leaning against my stretcher. In his garbled French he told me his life story. He'd been married to a Polish girl. She had died bearing their first child, a baby boy who had died too. After that he couldn't bear to stay at home any longer. That's why he was always sad and often seemed angry. But he had a heart of gold. When we were on leave, whenever he saw children he bought them candy and any other good things to eat he could find. Then when he was alone in his room he took out a picture of his wife that he carried in a special pocket on the inside of his belt and cried like a baby. Whenever I saw him in this state, I gave him something to drink and tried to cheer him up, for he was a very good soldier. Very brave and a first-class gunner. We nicknamed him the Airplane Shooter.

At the Hospital in Barcelona

At THE STATION in Barcelona my stretcher had scarcely been set down on the platform when for no apparent reason a crowd of photographers and journalists started firing questions about my wound. Then I was taken to the Sangre Hospital in the Calle Tallere. I was worried about the Czech. They told me he had been taken to the Karl Marx Barracks to rest.

At the hospital I was put in one of the rooms reserved for officers of the International Brigade. There were four of us: a Pole whose hands were horribly hacked up, a German whose leg had been cut off, and a Mexican wounded in the leg and the arm. Every few minutes a very pretty nurse would come and ask us if we wanted anything, and then bring it to us. At night a male nurse watched over us. He was an old Andalusian, always smiling. When we couldn't sleep he told us stories to help the time pass. He knew that I was worth spending time on, as my drawer was always full of good things. The Mexican was a devil; despite the fact that he could hardly move with a broken arm and leg, he gesticulated, talked and sang. The Pole was the most unfortunate. A grenade had gone off in his hands. The doctors did the best they could but his hands were tied in position high above his head. I was the only one in the room who could get around a bit. When the Pole was thirsty, I stepped out of bed and gave him a drink from the neck of the bottle of sparkling wine which we each got every morning. Then I got so I couldn't sleep in my bed. It was too good, too soft. I pulled off the cover and slept under the bed on the tiles. When the Andalusian nurse came he wanted me to get back in bed. I gave him tobacco to make him let me alone, but he said he'd be punished if they found me. So I let him put me back on the bed.

Four doctors came to examine me: an Englishman, a Frenchman, a Spaniard and a Pole. The shell fragment was deeply embedded in my thigh. It must have been very close to a nerve. They were afraid that in taking it out they would cut the nerve. The Frenchman, the Pole, and the Spaniard said it would be necessary to amputate the leg. Fortunately the Englishman said no: he would take care of me. He cleaned the wound with a long metal rod wrapped in cotton. Then he poured in a liquid that looked like water but burned like fire. It was torturing; I ground my teeth, I twisted, but I didn't scream; the doctors couldn't believe it. They worked without anesthetics as the hospital didn't have much of a supply and had to hold back on using them.

The food was better than a hotel's, and we even had imported delicacies. They brought me French books. Every afternoon I was visited by delegations of men and women from all countries: French, Swiss, English, etc. I refused the gifts they wanted to give me as I already had everything in my drawer; cigarettes, chocolates, and candy. I'd been given a beautiful pipe in which I smoked American tobacco. Each morning the nurse brought me a bottle of sparkling wine.

The fourth day I had a visit from Commissar Tito. He was accompanied by a Spanish colonel and a dozen officers from other countries. They brought me a Republican flag, red flowers and sugared almonds. Then I was rolled into a big room. Between the rows of beds of the wounded a platoon of the XVth International Brigade presented arms in my honor. Facing me were the Mexican, my Dutch orderly and the Czech. The colonel spoke of all our deeds and named all the comrades who had died for the Republic. Then I was lifted up and stood supported by two French officers while the colonel pinned on me the Bronze Medal of the Spanish Republic and the Medal of Merit of the Ebro. Then he named me staff lieutenant and gave me the stripes. The Mexican, who had been a lieutenant, received a captain's stripes and the Dutchman and the Czech got sergeants' stripes. After the ceremony a good meal was served to all the wounded. All the while the journalists had been taking photos. The next day they brought me a newspaper. I saw my photo, along with a big article telling of our heroic exploits.

At the end of the week, I started walking by pushing a chair. I'd been forbidden to get up, but my desire to walk overcame my physical weakness. The nurse, María Lacanca, had become a good friend. Her mother came to visit me, and also her little daughter. She was four years old and talked like a book. She was terrific; she kissed me, jumped on my bed and told me stories about mama, which mama fortunately didn't hear, as little ones tell the truth without knowing it.

Another week and I was walking with a cane. Then I went to visit the wounded in their rooms; I interpreted for them and shared my delicacies with them. Everyone called me the Frenchman. About every two hours there were aerial bombardments. We didn't pay any attention to them anymore. A bomb fell in the kitchen courtyard but we ate that day as usual.

One day the nurse brought me a splendid officer's uniform. She had sewn on the stripes but hadn't yet found ribbons for the decorations. Every afternoon my comrades came to visit. We talked of the bad moments and marveled that we were still alive. The Mexican said he was having a great time; he knew some good places for drinking and some for women. He had a girl friend, a gentle halfbreed Portuguese from Angola. The Dutchman and the Czech were always together. They took life seriously. They always walked in the areas most often attacked by planes. Their pleasure was watching the planes and the ships in the port.

Then the time came when I could walk outside the

hospital. I went to the nurse's house. María Lacanca was a Catalan from Barcelona. She was an anarchist, a real militant; she herself had killed her husband, who was a Fascist. When she finished her duties each day at two o'clock, we went walking. She wasn't afraid. Even when the sirens warned of an air raid we went on as though it was nothing and the little girl did the same.

One afternoon I went to the movies with my three friends. We were sitting quietly waiting for the film to start, when a Catalan sitting behind us who thought I didn't understand his language started abusing the internationals. I heard him say to his neighbor: *"Los intragero, qui viene asez aqui, no puede vise a pueblo, c'esr comme todo la bueno."* The Dutchman understood by my look but I checked myself and acted as though I didn't understand. But the Catalan repeated the thing, and this time the Mexican heard. I got up, whirled around and threw a punch at the man. The Dutchman, seeing his friend in a pinch, jumped on the Catalan. The Dutchman was an experienced fighter; he twisted the man's arm into his back with one hand and with a single blow sent him flying through the air. The Catalan fell on an onlooker. The police arrived. The Catalan's neighbor, who hadn't moved from his seat, said I was right. We went out to explain. The police wanted to take us to the station. The Mexican told them who we were and I showed them my decorations. They saluted us and we went back to the film.

The "Forest of Peace"

I STAYED at the hospital a few more days and then I was sent to convalesce at Las Planas, a large resort hotel on a mountain near Barcelona. There were convalescents there from all the International Brigades, which meant we were with people of all nationalities.

We each had a nice room. We led a pasha's life with nothing to do; they even made our beds. We could take a little train down to Barcelona, so there weren't many people at the hotel during the day. Many went to Barcelona in the mornings, and the rest passed their time in a whorehouse near the station where there were seven young and pretty girls who charged ten pesetas a throw.

The hotel was surrounded by forest. Lots of people camped under the trees. Others stood in line at the kitchen door at the back of the hotel to get a little food.

That surprised me. In Barcelona you saw poverty but there was food everywhere: nut sellers on the street corners; snacks of broad beans, shrimp, snails, ham, etc. in the taverns; and plenty of wine. And at the front there was so much of everything that it was a real waste. You could have walked off with anything; no one paid any attention. It was badly handled, as in the case of the trucks: at the front there were never enough, while Barcelona was full of new ones driving around without much to do.

The second week I was officer of the guard. In the afternoons I went to the forest and talked with the civilian refugees. I asked them about the state of their families, why they had come up here, why they didn't have anything to eat in Barcelona. A few seemed a bit suspect to me, but the majority were in a lamentable situation. I had noticed a pretty gypsy, about twenty years old, dressed in old but clean clothes. She sat beside her empty basket. She said for three days now she had waited all day and received nothing. I thought perhaps she was too proud to stand in the line. Or perhaps the other women mistreated her. I asked her name: it was Rosita. Her father was a paralytic in a wheelchair. They had no more money and for three days had eaten only half-rotten oranges. She gathered them on the beach after they had been thrown away into the sea.

After asking everybody a few questions I came back with quite a bit of information. I did some thinking: there were a hundred and twenty in the hotel but only eighteen ate here at noon. Where did the extra rations go? After investigating I realized that the chef was cheating people: he gave food to some but not to others, he played favorites. And the officer of the guard before me did some good distributing a few rations of stew and bread, but for the most part the uneaten rations had stayed in the cellar to rot.

As the responsible officer it was up to me to bring some order to this mess. The next morning I took several officers from the hotel and we went to see the forest people. First I told them there would be no more lines at the kitchen door. Each morning five of our men would come for their baskets and bring them back later filled with cold food. They were to eat in the forest. I had benches and planks brought and set them to work making tables, civilians and military alike. The women went to get dishes. I don't know how they did it, but they brought back two hundred metal plates.

Around eleven I assembled the whole group. I told them each day four men and ten women would be assigned work as helpers in the kitchen. They would peel potatoes, wash dishes and do all other necessary chores. Yelling and fighting were prohibited in the forest under penalty of expulsion. I named a man and two women to be in charge, and told them several officers from the hotel would sit at the dinner tables. Counting the children, there were three hundred people to feed. I ordered a quart of wine per adult. In overseeing so much food I rather lost my appetite. But I sat at the old people's table, and watching them eat with so much pleasure made me enjoy eating too.

The baskets were sent back filled with bread, dried beans, rice, even candy and chocolate that had piled up at the hotel during the last three months. Then I gave notice that they would not have to bother bringing their baskets up to the forest. Each was to give his city address and a truck from the hotel would make deliveries every day in Barcelona.

In the following days the forest filled with civilians and even soldiers from the surrounding area. Word had spread quickly in Barcelona. They ate and ate; everyone laughed, danced and sang. In spite of the fact that the number of people doubled everyone had his share and I even had food left over. Word spread among the merchants and peasants of the region and they all brought contributions: flour, sausage meat, tomatoes, eggplants, even some little pigs and goats. That touched me most of all, to see these peasants and merchants giving with a good heart.

The first days I stayed in the forest to keep an eye on things, I spent my time playing with children, always followed by the gypsy girl, who never left me. Finally I sent an automobile to pick up her father and had him put in a room near mine on the ground floor of the hotel. Each day a soldier pushed his wheelchair for a walk in the forest. Everyone was happy. They baptized the camp the "Forest of Peace" and called me "the Frenchman who is Chief of the Forest of Peace."

When my week as officer of the guard was over, I went down to Barcelona to find my friends at the Karl Marx Barracks. We went back to the camp with two accordions, three guitars and a banjo. That night we had a hell of a party. The Mexican danced with his half-breed girl friend. Everybody made a lot of noise and felt cheerful and happy.

Things went on like this for a month. But even though I could walk well enough, my leg still hurt inside. I was sent to the hospital in Vich, where they gave me electric massage treatments. When these were finished I was sent to Mataró, a little town on the sea eighteen miles from Barcelona in the direction of France. There I lived like a prince in a château, but I longed for my friends and the Forest of Peace.

One day I got the use of an automobile and I went

back to Las Planas. Nothing was left. The hotel was occupied by a general staff. I was politely received and invited to stay for dinner. Afterwards I went to the kitchen. I recognized two women who had worked there in my time. I asked them about the gypsy girl; she had gone back to the city with her father. It seemed she had found a job keeping house for a colonel.

I went back to Mataró, saddened by the empty forest. The next day I went to Barcelona with the truck. I took along a case of canned goods, packages of cakes and ten loaves of bread. The driver was a very nice black. I told him our story. He made the rounds of the old addresses. I didn't find anyone. The people had moved; where were they? No one knew. How could something so well arranged, something that had made everybody happy, be so quickly destroyed? It seems that those who work for the people can't be with them when they have the chance!

I did have the luck to find Rosita. I got a week's leave. I spent the nights in her big bed and the days roaming around Barcelona with my friends from the Karl Marx Barracks.

When I returned to Mataró a captain from the general staff ordered me to return immediately to Barcelona.

Last Combat
on the Ebro

AT GENERAL STAFF they explained that the Nationalists had attacked to retake the positions we'd conquered beyond the Ebro. Our troops, overwhelmed, had
withdrawn before a holocaust of bombardments. I was
given a free hand to form a company. As soon as we
were ready we were to go immediately to the front, to a
sector I knew well, the sierras de Pandols and Caballs.

I went to the Karl Marx Barracks and called my comrades together. First I found García, the Mexican;
Eureka, the Czech; and Mac, the Dutchman. Then the
Belgian Verterent who had returned after a long con-
valescence. I rounded up eleven veterans of other International Brigades who had stayed in Barcelona.*
I took two trucks and loaded three machine guns and
ammunition. Each of us carried four pineapple grenades, a large-caliber automatic pistol and a dagger. The

---

*After Munich, the positions taken by France and England
compelled Stalin to alter his political attitude towards Hitler and
Fascism; he demanded that foreign volunteers withdraw from
the Spanish war. The last engagement in which the XVth International Brigade participated was the English battalion's 22
September battle outside Gandesa. V.G.

Dutchman and I each had one dagger on our belt and another up our sleeve. We had our rucksacks and canteens. The Mexican took a liter gourd for wine. One truck carried all our supplies: tents, blankets, plenty of explosives, canned food and milk, three sacks of black bread, biscuits and a case of tobacco. We climbed into the other truck and were on the road without delay.

That evening we arrived in Falset. The town had been bombed. We left it and camped in an olive orchard near an abandoned farm.

Early in the morning the captain came and gave me my orders. The bridge had been bombed and I had to wait. When the repairs were finished I had the trucks cross one at a time, the men on foot behind them as the bridge cables weren't very solid. By daybreak we had crossed the river and we advanced with our rucksacks full and our blankets slung over our shoulders. A company of Republican soldiers followed behind; their officers were under my command. I took two of their men, Aragonese, as liaison.

We went through Asco and marched on, resting twenty minutes every two miles. The company officers were astonished at this and said we had to go faster. I explained that a man who went into combat tired was dead from the start. My men advanced guerrilla style on each side of the road; the soldiers behind marched in single file five yards apart. We marched the whole morning. About two in the afternoon a plane flew over. It dived at the road bombing and strafing. I lay flat behind a pile of gravel. A bomb exploded on the other side and I was covered with gravel. My head was bleeding but it wasn't serious. By bad luck the Mexican had an arm torn off. A Frenchman and two Italians had been killed, and two other Frenchmen were gravely wounded. Behind us the company had three dead and nine wounded. A half hour later two ambulances came for the wounded. The stretcher bearers made a dressing for my forehead and covered the bandage with a piece of khaki shirt so it would be less visible.

We set off again and came to a large woods. I had the company take cover in it. They waited while I went on reconnaissance. I advanced guerrilla style with my men toward the top of the hill. Halfway up I sent the Dutchman back to the company with orders to join us. Everything was quiet. We rested.

All at once one man, then ten, then twenty hurled themselves at us from the summit, running like madmen. They were unarmed. We stopped them. They said that the enemy had taken two positions and were advancing in large numbers. First the Moroccans, then legionnaires, and in the rear the Civil Guardsmen collecting prisoners. Meanwhile the company had joined us. I ordered them to go up through the forest to the left and try to get to the top of the hill before the enemy. I was going to advance straight ahead.

Once we came out of the trees it was like a big staircase climbing up. The peasants here cultivated the earth in terraces on the hillside. Every ten to fifteen yards there was a wall to hold in the earth. They were like steps three to five feet high. We weren't two hundred yards from the top when Republican soldiers came pouring over in disorder. They yelled, "Here they come!" I had my men form a line behind one of the walls. We set up the three machine guns. I sent a liaison to the company with orders to deploy along the walls and not enter in action until we were man to man; then they were to spring up and take the enemy from behind. We waited. Suddenly shells began falling like hail in front of us. Then I gave the order to advance through the shells and not retreat as the enemy would lengthen the range when their troops got to the top. On my left I saw my liaison join the company. The captain understood. The whole company moved forward and got in position about fifty yards from us. We were twenty yards from the top when the enemy fell on us. They came in bunches. It was the Moroccans. We let them come right up to us and only had to lift our heads to fire point-blank with rifles and machine guns. Then we climbed up the walls and advanced with grenades. On the left the company came out and attacked them on the flank. It was a massacre. The legionnaires, good soldiers, tried to disengage themselves but we threw ourselves at them and quickly dispersed them with our grenades. Now it was we who ran down the other side of the hill, driving the Civil Guardsmen before us. When our men saw the enemy retreating they stopped their flight, picked up weapons and joined us. I sent the Dutchman with two Aragonese to look for reinforcements on the road as we had to keep the enemy from regrouping. When we got to the bottom of the hill we liberated about a hundred prisoners the Civil Guardsmen had collected. There was no shortage of weapons; they were everywhere among the dead. That gave us another company. We advanced three miles without stopping. We came on a column of mortarers on muleback and took them without a fight. There was hardly any enemy reaction now, just a few shells here and there. They didn't know exactly where we were. We took up two positions, well situated with good trenches. But we were overextended, with too few men: I decided to stay there and wait for reinforcements.

I counted up my platoon: Verterent the Belgian had been killed by a bullet in the head in the beginning of the action. Of the new ones, six were dead and one wounded. We were the old three, myself, the Czech and the Dutchman, who I hoped would return soon. Captain González's company had had its losses but he had also picked up a lot of men. All the trenches seemed to be filled with new, well-armed soldiers. But they were hungry and thirsty and so tired they could hardly stand up. The enemy had recovered and began firing at our positions. But they didn't do any damage; the Moroccans had dug good trenches, well designed to provide shelter. The Czech and I were beginning to get worried about the Dutchman when he appeared followed by a major and several officers leading well-supplied reinforcements. They had come to relieve us. The major had biscuits, wine, water and cigarettes passed around. Refreshed, we started back down towards the road. We got there just as five of our tanks went by, to help defend the conquered positions. Then came a file of prisoners going to the rear where trucks would take them to the other side of the river. We arrived just in time to meet the liaison motorcyclist from general staff. He had an order for me saying to go a mile farther on and wait for new reinforcements in a grove of fig trees near a demolished house. We went and were pleasantly surprised to find a truck waiting for us with enough cold food for three days, and wine and cigarettes. We only had to reach out our arms for figs and grapes.

We waited there for two days, always on the alert as enemy planes passed over four or five times a day. They strafed the woods; then they came back to drop incendiary bombs that fell very gently, suspended from tiny parachutes.

The third day the reinforcements arrived, if you could call them that: a lieutenant with seven men from the XVth International Brigade, and behind them thirty-three Catalan peasants wearing corduroy and berets, all unarmed. One was a big man who seemed to be their leader. I asked him where they came from. He said they were all from Corbera; they had had to come or be treated as deserters if they refused. I asked if they knew how to use a gun. He said they had never fought in the war.

The lieutenant left, leaving me a paper from general staff. It was an order to occupy positions in the Sierra de Caballs.

We left. I led my ridiculous troops through the woods and the little roads I knew so well and once again I came to the head of the gorge. We rested in one of the caves. They had been cleaned out and fixed up as shelter for the troops. I found a major from general staff. I showed him my orders and explained my feeling about these peasants, who inspired no confidence at all. I was sure they'd slip off as soon as they had a chance. The major said that when I arrived at my position I would find a company which would take them in charge. After that I would have freedom of operation.

We spent the night and left about four: I wanted to

cross the plain before daybreak. The Catalans went slowly. They always had an excuse for stopping. I put the seven Internationals in the rear to keep an eye on them and push them on. We came to the end of the gorge. All was quiet, only a few rifle shots on the right. We crossed guerrilla style with the peasants in single file. Day broke as we reached the foot of the sierra. No one was there and we heard nothing. That seemed suspicious. The sierra positions appeared to be abandoned. I ordered a rest before the climb up. Pretending I had to relieve myself, I went behind a rock and undressed. There was a pair of Nationalist pants with wooden buttons in my rucksack. I put them on with my khaki shirt. Then I hid all my things, papers, uniform, rucksack, and canteen, under some rocks. I had my automatic and dagger on my belt and my throwing knife in my sleeve.

I gave the order to advance. I was in front with my ten men, and the peasants followed on the right. I ordered their leader to hold them twenty yards from the summit until I signaled them to go into the trench. I had no trouble finding the connecting trench. In the trench itself there was no one. No arms except for a case of grenades in a shelter. I advanced to look at the other side of the sierra in the distance, though without my binoculars, which I had left under the rocks. I saw no one and heard no firing. I went back to the trench to signal the peasants. There was still no one there. I went into the trench and hadn't gone fifty yards when suddenly I saw a troop of Carlists coming. There were about a hundred and they carried a white Monarchist flag. The leader of the Catalan peasants came up to my side. I jumped over the edge of the trench and found myself in front of a big Red Beret who had me at the point of his tommy gun. With my arms in the air, I threw myself to the ground and let my knife fly. The Carlist got it in the chest. He fell firing a burst that didn't hit me. I left, running on the side of the trail. I heard a machine gun firing bursts from behind a rock. I circled around the rock. It was an Italian firing on the trench to keep anyone from getting out. The trap was well set. I approached him at a walk as though I was one of theirs. I lay next to him and he told me to hand him ammunition drums. While he was firing I planted my dagger between his neck and shoulder and tore away the machine gun. I got up. I saw the Czech coming on the run. He had stayed at the entrance to the trench to cover us. He had fired his whole drum but the others were already prisoners. I gave him the machine gun and he went to set it up on its tripod behind a rock.

I started off down the sierra on the enemy's side. If you run away, you ought to run forward. I came to a small cave containing an antitank cannon guarded by two Moroccans. I killed them with my pistol. That emptied the pistol, and I threw it in a thicket. Now I looked for a hole to hide in. But a little farther down I ran into a group of officers. I went ahead calmly and told them I was lost. The commander asked me the name of my regiment. I gave him the number of one of our companies. One officer had drawn his revolver; the commander spoke to him, offered me a cigarette and told me to follow them. We walked a bit and they handed me over to some Civil Guardsmen who put me with the other prisoners. They tied my hands behind my back and a

Civil Guardsman slapped me as hard as he could. The Guardsmen pushed us on and we came to a place where there were Moroccans. We passed in front of them and one took out his *gourmia,* a kind of curved saber, grabbed one of the prisoners by the hair and cut off his head with a single blow. A Carlist officer ran up too late. He hit the Moroccan in the back with a rifle butt and yelled, "You savage bastard, these are Spaniards!" But the Moroccan went back to his ranks laughing. We were in an area closed off by a huge boulder. I saw all the internationals of my platoon except for the Czech lined up against it with their hands tied behind their backs. In front of them were about twenty of our Catalan peasants, all armed with tommy guns, laughing and smoking cigarettes. The Guardsmen made us halt. The Catalans got in position in front of our comrades and at their leader's signal, they shot them with their tommy guns. Then they threw their bodies in a pit already piled with corpses. One of the Guardsmen dragged over the body of the decapitated prisoner and threw in the head with a laugh. Then the Guardsmen led us off again with insults and kicks.

We marched an hour and came to a highway full of convoys. Not far off we could see the town of Gandesa. A squadron of airplanes suddenly appeared in the sky. They were ours. They strafed the convoys and fired grenades. We wanted to get away from the road but the Civil Guardsmen made us lie on the ground and held us there at gunpoint. Then a squadron of Italian fighters and German Junkers arrived. Our planes counterattacked. In order to fight better, the bombardiers jettisoned all their bombs, which fell all around, causing panic. It was the biggest aerial battle I ever saw. I counted thirty enemy planes and at least twenty-five of ours shot down in flames. We saw Nationalists running after the pilots who landed in parachutes and when they were ours they nailed them with their bayonets, even though they were Spaniards.*

When the battle was over, the Guardsmen tied our feet and loaded us like sacks in a truck. Then when we came to Gandesa they locked us up, still bound, in an olive oil factory with guards inside and out.

*Foreign pilots had been withdrawn by this time. V.G.

CAPTIVITY

November, 1938 – July, 1940

Disciplinary Battalion 827

A<small>FTER A NIGHT</small> on the train, we stopped at a large station. It was Zaragoza. We were led to a barracks and all forty of us were locked in a room, still crowded together as we had been in the railroad car. We were left there, standing, all day and all night. We gasped for breath; the room stank as a corner began to fill with excrement. In the morning we were taken out and lined up in three ranks with other prisoners in the courtyard. We waited a long time. Then a Civil Guard colonel arrived. He was a small man with a big moustache and he carried a baton. Twenty Civil Guardsmen were stationed in the courtyard with a machine gun pointing at the prisoners. The colonel made a sign and an officer stepped forward and read us a report: during the fighting in which we had been made prisoners, the Reds had killed two majors, one captain, three lieutenants, eighteen sergeants and twenty-one corporals of the Nationalist army. When the officer finished reading, the colonel passed along our ranks and from time to time designated a prisoner with his baton. The Civil Guardsmen followed, took these men from the ranks and stood them to one side. As the colonel designated the prisoners, he counted aloud; before commencing he had shouted that he needed seventy. When he came to

111

me, he looked at me and put the baton on the shoulder of the man next to me. When it was over he stood in front of us, shouted, "Now justice will be done!" and raised his arm in the Fascist salute. The seventy were lined up against the wall. The Civil Guardsmen fired their tommy guns. Then an officer of the Civil Guard walked along and put a revolver bullet in the head of each fallen man. The wall was all splattered with blood. Two trucks with red crosses on their tarpaulins drove up. The soldiers threw the corpses in. The show was over and we were locked up again. But this time, with three comrades, I was put in a room furnished with four straw-mattressed iron beds, a table and a chair.

Towards evening a priest came in. He sat at the table, opened a large book and questioned us one by one. He wrote down the place of birth, relatives, and circumstances of entering the army. I was the last; I gave my real name, risking nothing as I had never lived in Spain. As address I gave Calle Tallere in Barcelona; no living relatives, I had lived with my mother but she was killed in the bombing. I spoke French because I had been raised in Marseille by one of my aunts who had married a Frenchman, M. Bouchez. They lived on the rue du Petits-Puits. I was mobilized with my age group in 1937 and had been in the 127th battalion* stationed at the Pueblo Nuevo barracks in Barcelona. Except for my name, everything I said was false. I had to keep all that in my head for surely I would have to repeat it many times.

---

*In order to stay alive Francisco had to conceal the fact that he had been in one of the International Brigades. V.G.

The priest left. They brought us bread, water and blankets. I passed the night as in a dream. It was a long time since I had slept in a bed.

The next morning they led us into a small courtyard where there were already some fifty prisoners. On one side a group of officers stood on a balcony. Some soldiers brought them pots and they began, laughing, to throw us *chorizos* (very highly seasoned red sausages) and dried sardines. The prisoners fought to grab them. One of the officers filmed the scene. I was so astonished that I missed my chance to grab something. Afterwards I did not regret it; towards evening all those who had profited from the distribution were almost crazed with thirst. Fortunately a priest brought them a little water.

We were locked in our room for two days. The morning of the third day, at four o'clock, we were awakened by a soldier who pulled my neighbor from his bed, made him dress and took him away without explanation. Twenty minutes later I heard a volley of shots and I understood: the comrade would not come back.

The next day we were all assembled in the large courtyard. They called the roll, then gave us each a large loaf of bread, a can of sardines, and a plate of boiled cabbage. Then we were formed into a column three abreast, and led out of the barracks.

When we arrived at the railway station we were told to get into a boxcar and we traveled all day and all through the night. Around ten in the morning the train stopped. They told us to get out. As we had been on our feet a day and a night packed one against the other, we could hardly stand up. We were loaded into trucks. The Basque prisoners recognized the country: we were in the environs of Bilbao. We got out in the courtyard of an old castle quite close to the sea. We were each given a metal plate, a spoon and an empty tin can. Our guards were Galician soldiers. They called the roll and divided us into three companies, selecting three leaders for each one. When that was finished they gave us each a roll, a plate of lentils, an orange and all the water we wanted. That caused a stampede: the water tasted so good we all but swallowed the faucet. Then each company was led to a large room. We were amazed to find military beds: an iron frame with a card bearing a number, three planks and a straw mattress. Each man was assigned a bed according to his number.

It was cold. We rested two days doing nothing and then the work began. The day started with an hour of singing. We were taught "Cara al Sol" and the stiff-armed Hitler salute. Then we were taken to the beach. We went into the water up to our waists and had to remove chunks of rock and put them on the shore. That lasted all morning. We came back in the afternoon and then had to throw the rocks back into the sea. They said it was to make our backs strong. By evening we were dead with fatigue. Soon our legs broke out with an itchy rash that became unbearable if you scratched. Woe to him who complained, for he had to swallow a dose of castor oil. If one of us fell at work and could not get up, he was shot with a rifle. One afternoon we buried two prisoners of our company in the sand at the edge of the sea.

Fortunately, after a few days we were put on a train again and found ourselves in Logroño. There we were taken to an old convent. The courtyard was full of prisoners. Civil Guardsmen and Fascist officers of all sorts went back and forth on the balconies. At noon we were taken to a large room with tables and benches. We sat down to eat. If someone had told me we would be served a plate piled high with fried potatoes, fried fish and a small beefsteak on the side I would never have believed it; but it happened. All this with a white bun, a big pastry, an orange, a glass of wine, and five cigarettes when we had finished. Strange that they treated us so kindly! Soon we would see why.

After eating, feeling quite content, we were led into the courtyard. Then they began to call us ten by ten, and each time the ten were taken to the upper story. My turn came. We were lined up in a corridor and called in one at a time. I entered a large apartment. Six officers were seated around a table. They were all smiling. One of them stood up, gave me his hand, asked me to sit down and asked for the usual information. I repeated all that I had said at Zaragoza. Another officer wrote. Then I was told to stand, still amiably; I was photographed and given my statement to sign. Another officer offered me a package of cigarettes, then I was led to another door and taken down into a different courtyard. The sorting was over.

That night we slept in a large room, pressed against each other on the floor without blankets. In the night a gypsy prisoner asked to go out to urinate. A Civil Guardsman accompanied him. The gypsy jumped him, choked him, took his revolver, put two bullets in his head and ran. In the corridor he encountered two more Civil Guardsmen. He killed one and wounded the other, who fired at him. With a bullet in his belly he still had the strength to get to the balcony. He jumped off and broke his head on the pavement below.

We didn't have to wait long. Two officers followed by many Civil Guardsmen entered the room. The officers lined us up. Then one of the officers took a riding crop and began to march up and down in front of us striking blows all around while yelling names like thief, assassin, criminal. That lasted an hour. When his rage had passed he had the Civil Guardsmen remove two of our number who had dared to talk back to him. At dawn they were shot.

We were taken to Mass and afterwards put in trucks which brought us to the camp Miranda Ebro. We slept on the ground in wooden huts. The next morning we woke up covered with fleas and lice. I didn't stop killing them all day. My shirt was full of them, and the pleats and seams of my pants, too. When the day began we were formed in ranks in the courtyard. A Civil Guard colonel walked up to a platform and all the while he was there we had to sing "Cara al Sol." It was the same in the afternoon, and again in the evening after supper. We were guarded by Galicians and soldiers from the Canary Islands who communicated only by hitting us for no reason. One morning, at roll call, the names of eighteen prisoners were called out and they were shot in front of us.

One morning, about a month later, I was ordered to step out from the ranks with some other prisoners. They set us apart and then took us to the showers in groups of six. We had to strip and throw our clothes into a cauldron. We had a shower and then a vaccination in the arm from a doctor. Then we were taken to a store where we were handed a metal plate, a spoon, a fork, two shirts, two pairs of socks, a cap with a T, a pair of heavy shoes, pants, jacket, sweater, sheet, blanket, bar of soap and a towel — all new. The clothes and shoes were too big for me. I exchanged them with a big man who had everything in my size. Then we were led on foot to the station. There they added a large loaf of bread, two cans of sardines, a can of beans with meat, a package of cigarettes, and had us get into the boxcars. Curiously, they did not close them; two soldiers escorted us in each car. The ones in mine were middle-aged men from the Canaries. They put down their rifles and right away began talking, smoking and joking with us. One of them smoked a pipe. The train stopped at a small station; we were allowed to relieve ourselves and get water. The commanding officer, also middle aged, even came along pouring out a little wine. The journey went on two days until we arrived in Guadalajara.

The camp there was made up of barracks surrounding a large hangar which had housed a dirigible, a *globo*. The camp was named for it. We spent the day looking around everywhere. Astonishingly, the soldiers put down their guns and came looking with us. We saw that they wanted to be our friends.

The next day we assembled in the middle of the grounds. We were six hundred prisoners. Autos arrived and officers got out and began to form us into companies. The commandant was a Catalan, a man of fifty-five to sixty. They formed six companies of a hundred men, each having two sergeants, two lieutenants, a captain and twenty-two soldiers for guards. We were each given a white armband with a large black T which we had to wear on our left arm. We were Disciplinary Battalion 827 of workers. Each company occupied a barracks. My company were almost all Basques. There were a few Andalusians and Catalans, ten men from Valencia and one from Alicante. The soldiers guarding us were mostly from the Canaries, with a few Galicians. The two sergeants were Andalusians; one lieutenant was from Santander and the other was an Andalusian. The captain of the company was from Madrid. One sergeant and the lieutenant from Santander were mean. The other officers and soldiers were very kind to us.

In my section of thirty men there were two other prisoners who like myself spoke French. We became friends at once. José Cortal was from Valencia, but his parents lived in Toulouse. The other was a Basque from Bilbao whose relatives were also at Toulouse. The one I confided in most was José Cortal; the other was more reserved and besides he was always with the mean lieutenant from Santander, so I spoke to him as little as possible, hoping to avoid drawing the lieutenant's attention.

Each company had its own kitchen with a separate one for the officers. The food was plentiful but bad because the officers and soldiers took the best of it first. Once a week the commandant came for inspection. He talked with us and on that day the food was better. There was more wine and even a dessert. Then the commandant left and things were the same again.

The first week they drove us crazy with marching in step, right face and so on. It was like a military school. We drilled so much that I think we could have paraded with the best soldiers in the army. Except that our arms were shovels and picks. And of course every morning and evening "Cara al Sol" with the arm raised in the Fascist salute.

One morning Sergeant Gil, an honest Andalusian, tall, lean, and a bit lame but always smiling, took my section and led us to the station. For three weeks we unloaded boxcars: sacks of cement, boards, materials for repairing bridges, etc. I formed a team with Cortal, two Basques and a tailor who had made suits in Barcelona.

Then one morning we were awakened very early. We folded up our clothes, put our sacks on our backs, left for the station and embarked on a freight train. We traveled all day and all night. We ate a roll, a can of tuna fish and a can of beans. And this time we had water: we had each received a quart canteen. We debarked in open country on the bank of a river, the Segre. We were lodged in an empty sheepfold, with the officers in an abandoned farmhouse. The kitchens were set up outdoors.

The next morning we were led to the river. Its bed was dry but was full of large stones. They gave us each a sledgehammer and put the whole company to work breaking stone. I quickly got blisters on my hands and fragments hit my legs and drew blood. By luck I was next to a man who had done this work all his life. He showed me how to do it: you hold the stone with the foot and look for the vein. You hit right on it, then hit the flat part and the stone falls apart in pieces. Trucks came to pick up the broken stone, doubtless to pave a road.

The food wasn't bad: lentils, dried beans, potatoes with mutton, vegetable soup and a half pint of wine. The commandant came often to check the meals. But at night we couldn't go out to get air and for our natural needs we had to ask the sentry. The third night Ramón, an Aragonese, asked to go out to relieve himself. He was a poor boy, a bit simple, who spoke little and did everything backwards. The non-coms hated him; they took his food and struck him with whips, and the lieutenant from Santander used to slap him, laughing gleefully. It made no difference. The blows didn't make him more intelligent; on the contrary he got worse and worse. The sentry took him to the riverbank. Ramón took down his pants, squatted, and all of a sudden rushed at the sentry butting him with his head. The sentry fell. Ramón seized the rifle and stabbed the sentry seventeen times with its bayonet. Afterwards, according to the man who told the tale, he ran across the riverbed and escaped. We all had to get up and the officers came and beat us with their riding crops. Then they took ten prisoners from Ramón's section and shot them in front of us at dawn on the riverbank. Then they made a speech. If one of us escaped, ten comrades of his section would be shot.

The gallant old commandant arrived as a result. He did not approve of the punishment, but the officers said that was the law of war: you kill and you are killed.

We stayed ten days, and then the trucks came and took us to La Olmeda de Jadraque, a village of the legion of Sigüenza. We found our gravel piled in heaps along the road which climbed in switchbacks up the mountain. We widened the road. The work was tiring because the red earth was clay and stuck to our feet. They gave us wheat bread white as snow. We stayed there twenty days, then we were transported with all our possessions to the village of Horna, some eleven miles away. We were lodged in a sheepfold and the kitchen was set up in the middle of the village square. Luckily there was a canal; we could bathe; our clothes were put through a steam laundry. We were clean.

Prisoners' Trades

A WEEK after our arrival in Horna, the commandant came to review our company. He asked each one his trade. When he came to me I said that I was a jack of all trades and master of none. He replied, "We'll see about that!"

Two days later the baker's wife came to ask if there was a baker-oventender among us. In this village the women made their loaves themselves and then brought them to the baker to be baked. The Fascists had put the baker in prison and his wife came to see the commandant. He thought of me. He had me brought in and said, "You who have plied all trades, do you know how to do that?" I didn't tell him I had been a baker with my Uncle Ramón in Algeria. You should never tell all you know or all you're thinking. I answered, "I'll try."

Early next morning I went to the oven. I made faggots of pine, then took out the embers and put them on the right side by the door and swept the bottom of the oven with a wet sack on a pole. When the women brought me their loaves, I marked each with a number on the iron baking sheet and asked, well browned or light? and I marked that too. Some brought shortbread, others cakes. The baker's wife gave me a bit of flour and I made some round and some crown-shaped loaves.

When I came back for dinner in the afternoon, I gave a loaf to Cortal and a large loaf to the section, who devoured it as if it had been cake. That evening I had supper with the baker's wife. Her cooking was good and there was plenty of wine. She gave me tobacco that the people of the village had hidden. I smoked very little but kept all she gave me to bring back to my section. A sentry was with us, and thanks to him I managed to sneak a bottle of good wine into camp which we drank in secret that night with the Basques.

There were few men left in the village. My section in addition to the road work lent a hand to the peasants with the heavy work in the fields. These people were very charitable; they were all peasants and small tradesmen, except for two landowners who owned almost all the fields. We all got along well and there was plenty to eat. There was a little church; the priest, a fat pig, reigned over the village. He had had almost all the men arrested. Only old men and Fascist leaders were left. The baker's wife was rather pretty, and not too old. But I didn't trust her; her tongue wagged too much. You often talk more than you should when your head lies on a pillow; and she was the kind of woman who told her priest everything.

I played the baker for thirty-five days. The wine and

food made us gay. In the evenings we laughed and sang, and everybody told stories of his town or village. We ended up knowing each other well and became good friends.

But in our situation nothing lasted very long. The trucks came for us one day and by evening we found ourselves in open country. We slept under huge olive trees. The soldiers and officers slept a bit further on in a big half-demolished farmhouse. We were free to walk in the fields but were forbidden to go past the road.

The next day was a day of rest for the medical visit. We went down to the farmhouse and stood in line waiting to see the doctor. Just as we were going in, a man pushed me to get in front. Cortal was beside me and I said in French, "Go ahead. You'll get a double dose and it's all free." The man did not understand, but the doctor had heard me. When my turn came, as he was examining me he asked me why I spoke French. I told him. He asked me if I knew how to read and write. I answered yes, but I made mistakes. Then he said, "I need an interpreter. Go look for the commandant." The doctor, a man of about thirty, was a Parisian who had volunteered to come treat the wounded in Spain. He had not chosen a side. When the war was over he stayed to treat the prisoners. As I went out I told the sergeant the doctor's order. The commandant arrived and had me go in with him to see the doctor. He explained, "I speak Spanish badly and my orderly has difficulty understanding my orders. I would like to have this prisoner with me. I will teach him to be a medic and he will be my interpreter." It was agreed on, and once again my life changed.

123

El Médico Francés

T HEY TOOK AWAY my shovel and my dirty clothes and gave me a new uniform. Then I joined the doctor in his big house. I was given a white apron, a large first-aid kit and a length of rubber tubing for stopping hemorrhages. I was shown the stretcher and a portable pharmacy neatly arranged in cases. Two aides from each company were assigned to me for carrying all these supplies when we were on the march.

While my section worked at rebuilding a bridge, I stayed with the doctor. He taught me many things about the medications and gave me a large book describing the various ailments. In the mornings I made the rounds with the doctor, in the quarters and in the work-yards, as the company was also repairing the roads in the region. When we finished the rounds, the doctor drove to a convent some seven miles from the camp which had been transformed into a hospital. The patients were mainly soldiers, but there was one ward for civilians. There were so few doctors that the Frenchman served other companies as well as my own, and on the way from one to the other he stopped off at country hospitals like this one. He was always on the road.

At the convent I visited the patients with him. At each wounded man he showed me how to make emergency dressings, and at each sick patient he showed me how to recognize a fever, look in the throat and tap the belly. Then there were consultations with civilians who often came a long way to have a chance to see a doctor. Many of these had only a sprained ankle, a dislocated knee or elbow, or a twist in their back. I told the doctor I knew something about treating these cases. I quickly put the nerves back in place. A good massage, hot compresses, a cataplasm of herbs I knew, and presto, my patients could turn their arms and legs again and were comfortable. The doctor was quite astonished; I told him it was a family gift, without giving too many details as I was supposed to have no relations in either France or Spain.

I slept in the pharmacy on a real bed with sheets and blankets. I ate at the mess hall but in the kitchen, and I got double ration. When I filled my plate for the second time, I took it to friends in my section. The soldiers didn't eat much better than the prisoners: always the same thing, potatoes with bones and dried vegetables. However, when the provisions for the battalion were unloaded, it was something to see. There were toasted barley, sugar, salt, preserves, whole truckloads of bread, cases of canned milk, quarters of beef and whole sheep with their heads. The officers' mess took the best and shared it with their friends for whom they held feasts. The cook in turn got his rake-off; his friends left with cans of oil and demijohns of wine! If it had all been distributed according to regulations, there would have been enough for all to eat well and in abundance. In my room,

I had three cases of canned milk for the sick who couldn't eat. Often the sergeant, the lieutenant or the captain would come in and take some cans. One morning I told the doctor of this traffic. He said, "They have no right. These cases were sent for the sick by the Red Cross. To get milk you have to have a paper signed by me or the commandant of the battalion." The commandant had his own cook who never took milk or provisions from the battalion. His food came from the general staff and he ate apart. But when he came to the battalion you noticed it right away: the food was better, there were fewer punishments. He was like a father whose coming we waited for. The doctor told him about the milk, and the commandant said in front of his officers that it was forbidden to enter the offices or private rooms of the infirmary and take anything without his permission or mine. Before everyone he appointed me health officer of the battalion and gave me a commission signed by the commanding general of Guadalajara. With this important paper I could go out day or night. He also gave me an armband marked with a red cross and a certificate as army medic. All the officers congratulated me, shook my hand and we drank good wine with cakes. The commandant said he was very pleased with me. When the officers had left the doctor asked the commandant to watch that my orders were obeyed. "I am responsible for him," he said. "I have found here a good servant of the sick. He is very skillful at treating displaced nerves and he is a good masseur. At the hospital he is in demand as he brings about many recoveries." Then the commandant told me, "Take good care of these papers. One day they may be of great service to you."

The doctor stayed another week with us. Then one day he left, leaving me everything: the pharmacy, the sick and the wounded. Unfortunately I couldn't do very much. I was often obliged to use the same thing for diverse ailments. But I had to separate the malingerers from the sick, and that bastard of a lieutenant from Santander who stuck his nose in everywhere was always around. He would have been very happy to catch me in a mistake. Apart from that I was well off: I had all I wanted to eat and could go out whenever I wanted. I had a good life. I visited the workyards and treated men on the spot, and as I had a lot to do I appointed Cortal and the Catalan tailor to aid me on my rounds. I had a big job, and often my rounds lasted through the night until two in the morning.

I was respected by everyone in the battalion and even by the people of the village. The prisoners felt that I did them good; for many who were not sick but only exhausted I ordered two or three days' rest and I was obeyed. But I was not a doctor and I had the worst-off patients evacuated to the hospitals.

Then it came time to move again and we found ourselves at Baseilla, in the province of Tarragona, where the company was to repair another bridge. It was a small town of four or five thousand inhabitants. There were two highways which crossed in the middle of the town. On one corner of the crossing there was a cinema. My section was lodged there, and I with my pharmacy was given a house nearby.

Here we were in Cataluña. It was the first time we had been in a town which had been on the Republican side throughout the war. We were more free, and there was less to fear from propaganda. We helped the peasants with their work in the fields, and often they and the townspeople came to visit us and drink a bit. The soldiers guarding us put their bayonets aside and drank with us. We were all together like a big family, soldiers, officers and prisoners, each doing his work. The political hatreds had eased up a bit, perhaps because we ate better and were better treated. Then too we were less fatigued: we did our work better and sometimes even took pleasure in it. We were like an engineering corps; we could even forget that we were a disciplinary company. Sunday afternoon the whole company had liberty. The prisoners quartered in the countryside dressed neatly and came to town to promenade on one of the wide avenues called *ramblas*.

Some even received visits from their relatives every Sunday. The inns were full of people and those who had their families invited the others to drink with them. Everyone was happy. When the good commandant came and saw all this, he could hardly believe his eyes. He was very pleased.

The cinema was large and very modern for a small town. It had a good stage with a curtain. That gave me the idea of putting on a show to entertain the company. So when making my rounds, I looked for singers, musicians and comedians. I got permission for them to come in the evenings with their guards who were glad to have this good luck. We rehearsed. I directed everything a bit and with our meager equipment we made things that appeared magnificent. I recalled my tour with the circus and put on a clown number. We made posters to invite the population. We borrowed benches and chairs. The day of the presentation, a Sunday, the cinema was full. The first row was filled by officers around the commandant. We even had unarmed Civil Guardsmen and a truckload of Carlist soldiers who were passing through. We put on Andalusian songs with guitars, Basque ensemble numbers, dances from various provinces of Spain and then the clown act in which I played Charlie Chaplin and also the "human ape." Everyone laughed and laughed. At the end there was a number that included all the performers with a paso doble for a finale. We got lots of applause and afterwards everyone congratulated us, soldiers and civilians alike. The town band was applauded for playing the sardanas and the commandant thanked the girls and women who helped with the decor and costumes. He was very pleased and gave the entire company liberty for the night. Then we all went out to drink together. You should have seen the Carlists passing the bottles to the prisoners and handing out cigarettes. When they had to leave, one of them even gave some pesetas to the prisoners so they could buy more drinks. Only the Civil Guardsmen stayed apart. Those bastards were always sent far from their own region and were ordered to keep together and never talk to the local population.

Afterwards we worked all night cleaning up the hall, washing the floor and the stage and putting the beds, which had been piled up in a corner, back in place. We slept a few hours and next day there was a happy surprise: work was halted for everyone and we had three days' rest while we awaited the trucks taking us to a new area.

After a long trip we unloaded at Sigüenza. This was a big town and the regimen was different: barracks, sentinels and night rounds. In the morning trucks came to pick up the prisoners and take them to the workyards. We rebuilt buildings, moved earth, repaired railway embankments and so on. I made my rounds in a van driven by a sergeant named Gil, who was very kind. We stopped often at the taverns. We had plenty of time as there were few sick and injured. Our health was better, and there were fewer accidents now that the workers knew their trades better. We remained twenty days and then it was a new departure.

The company boarded a small train at the Sigüenza station. We occupied all the cars except one at the end reserved for civilians. We rode all day and in the evening we came to Soria. There everything was different again. We were in a large city, the capital of a province that had always been occupied by the Nationalists. Our reception was not the same. There wasn't even a cat in the street. As soon as our column advanced down a street, the doors banged as though we were bringing the plague, the Red plague. No one was permitted to leave the barracks and the next day the commanding colonel made a speech to remind us that we were prisoners subject to all the usual regulations.

I set up my infirmary in a separate, large room. I had spoken to our commandant and succeeded in getting Cortal and the Catalan to lodge with me. Through the window opening on the street we could see the city. Soria was a capital of priests; you saw only churches, chapels and convents. There was always a bell ringing somewhere and the streets were black with priests and nuns. You seldom saw any other civilians. The next day was Sunday. We had to dress neatly and were taken to

Mass, well surrounded by our guards. On leaving the church we had to march in step singing "Cara al Sol."

On Monday the company sent sections in all directions to various workyards. After I finished my rounds with my Red Cross armband and my papers in my shirt pocket, I went to visit the hospital. The reception was painful. They followed me around like dogs ready to kill. At each door I was asked for my papers and looked up and down. I finally came to the dispensary. I asked to be supplied with dressings, ether, aspirin, peroxide, etc. They told me I would have to give an account of my sick and injured. I had all that in my notebook and I showed it to them. I waited an hour and at last they brought me a large carton of all sorts of supplies, including things I had not asked for. I took the package and then two priests came up who spoke to me in a friendly way and said they wanted to come with me. When we arrived at the barracks, I invited them to come in and showed them my room and the pharmacy where everything was already well arranged. Then I took them into the hall where the beds of my sick and injured were. Both were astonished. They told me they hadn't expected all this and invited me to come back to the hospital the next day. "Ask for Father Matías."

The following day I went to the hospital. I was taken to a large office where I saw Father Matías. He was in charge of all the priests in the hospital. Then I understood everything when he asked me what I did to restore the nerves and massage paralyzed muscles. I told him, and he asked if I would try to treat some of the sick here. I said yes and he gave me what I needed. We went into a ward where there were many patients, men, women and children. I examined them while some of the staff brought the medicine I needed: alcohol, resin, bay leaves and so on. I rapidly put some nerves back in place in the hands and ankles of some of the children. Two old people afflicted with rheumatism I treated with massages and hot compresses. I worked up a good sweat treating everyone. When I was ready to leave they brought me a big carton full of sausages, chocolates and candy. There was also a whole ham, two big loaves of white bread, cakes, five bottles of good wine, a bottle of anisette and a picture of the Holy Virgin on top. Two soldiers came to carry the carton and four priests escorted me back. At the barracks they asked to see the commandant. They explained what I had done and wanted me to come back every afternoon to treat the patients who would be gathered together in a special ward. The commandant was very proud and he gave his permission.

So every day after my rounds I visited the hospital. No more formality or demands to see my papers now. I was given lunch with more than I could eat and all the wine I wanted. Next to the ward reserved for patients I had a small room with all that I needed to prepare my remedies. I hammed it up a little, pretending to have secret recipes with all my herbs and potions. Afterward I visited the patients. Some could leave right away with their nerves put back in place; the next day they would be able to use their arms and legs. Others I kept a night or two. For these I gave massages and made hot cataplasms with herbs, having them changed every three hours. Some arrived bent and left straight, others could walk better than they ever had before. I had about eighty percent success. The priest and sisters couldn't believe their eyes. They spoke of miracles; as for myself,

I thought of my grandmother who would have been very pleased to see all this, all these people who could get up and walk and who embraced me with tears. The story spread around the city from priest to priest, and then into the countryside. They stood in line to be healed. Often the case was not serious and the patient was relieved at once: a wrist or shoulder put back in place and he left "healed," as they called it; and the priests got their money out of the deal as well.

One Sunday I took Cortal, the Catalan tailor, and another Catalan, a wood merchant who had money and shared it, to the hospital with me. They were all astonished. The priests gave us dinner in a private room with a sister to serve us — and what a dinner! And what wine! I left the others at the table and went to make my rounds.

I had been at the hospital a fortnight. I was called *el médico francés*, the French medic. They gave me a pile of books and I studied a lot of antiquated medicine in old books that discussed the use of plants. And then one day it was time to leave.

The commanding colonel went to see our commandant. He wanted the French medic to remain at the hospital. Our commandant would not hear of it.

"What! When we arrived you didn't want to see us and now you want to take my medic! I need that man. He can do anything I ask."

The colonel replied that he would get me a good position at the hospital, that I would have all the papers I needed to practice my trade, and that one day I would be freed. The commandant would not listen; he wanted to keep me.

The good man really liked me. He was a count and

had a château near Barcelona. He would be able to retire soon. Then he was going to take me with him and I would be the manager of his holdings. "You are alone, and so am I; you will be like my son." I couldn't tell him that I had my family in France, and that in the back of my head I had the notion of going back to them.

It was time to go. You should have seen the station! It was filled with sisters and priests and Father Matías was there too. All the women kissed his hand. Civilians were everywhere with gifts. Our officers couldn't believe this fine farewell. The colonel and then Father Matías embraced me on the quai and when the train left, without anyone telling us to, we sang "Cara al Sol."

I Become an Ironworker

AT GUADALAJARA the battalion occupied the Maestranza, the trades school. It was like a large barracks surrounded by walls. Workshops lined the sides; in the center was the personnel building where the entire battalion with its five hundred men and its forty-eight soldiers and officers were lodged. The infirmary was a large hall with two good-sized rooms in the rear: one for the pharmacy, the other for myself and my two aides, Cortal and the Catalan. It was amazing how they had filled out, now that they had plenty to eat. I sent them to install the beds with the sick men in the large hall. I set up my materials in the pharmacy: my pots of salve and bottles of herbs and leaves, as I now treated often with plants and remedies of my own making. The next day two nurses came, French nuns. They were old women and already they were full of respect for *el médico francés*.

I didn't have much to do; once I had looked after the needs of the sick I made a tour of the workshops.

Guadalajara had been on the front line not far from Madrid. Now that combat had ceased, the Nationalists were busy recovering the iron left on the battlefields. All day long trucks came to unload skeletons of cars, trucks, old farm machines, motorbikes, bicycles, scrap metal — everything metal that could be found in the ruins of a countryside which had been bombarded for two years. There were even burnt-out tanks.

Teams were put to work sorting out this heap of scrap iron. It was piled up all around and if it continued like this we wouldn't be able to move. At the foundry the master founder was going mad; it was the same in the carpentry shop where they were salvaging everything made of wood. The work was dangerous. I was going to have many injured and burned, because they would forget to empty the gas tanks of the vehicles and often the tanks caught fire and exploded.

The battalion also furnished workers for the factories of the city. Sometimes when I finished my duties at the infirmary I would go into the city.

Among my sick I had a smith from Alicante, a good worker but a cold man. He received a lot of money but never gave any to his comrades, and he smoked all the time but never offered anyone a cigarette. One day when I lifted up his straw mattress I found a rucksack filled with tobacco and cigarettes. I took them all, went into the dormitories and put a package of tobacco or cigarettes on each bed. That raised a ruckus when the prisoners came back from work, and when the smith realized his treasure had been distributed he told everyone he was going to complain to the officer of the day. The commandant called me in; when I told him what happened he began to laugh. "That's fine. You gave him a good lesson." Then the commandant said, "Until now you have always won: I asked you to be a baker and you made good bread; I asked you to treat the sick and you cured them. Now I'm on a new spot. Scrap iron is coming into the Maestranza so fast that as you can see we don't know where to put it. But almost nothing is coming out of the foundry; the woodsheds are full but they can never find good planks or rafters. I have been put in charge of the whole enterprise. But even if I am a good soldier, I am not a good laborer, and I am on the point of losing this battle. Could you help me win it, you the jack of all trades?"

I didn't tell him I had begun my apprenticeship in a shipyard and that I knew much more about the treatment of metals than about the treatment of the sick. But I told him, "The trouble with this setup is bad organization. If I plan the work for you, if you give the orders I tell you to give, and if you give me the responsibility for all the scrap iron, I'm sure I can win the battle for you."

The commandant happily said, "It's a deal." He gave

me the list of items that the Maestranza was supposed to produce. I was to make my plan according to that. The following day I was to report and the plan would be discussed with the officers.

The next day, when I explained what we had to do, they were not all pleased. To give the responsibility for running the works to a "Red" didn't seem like good policy. The commandant said, "Things are going very badly. We can't go on like this. It's not an officer's job, it's a worker's. If *el francés* can straighten the business out, let's give him a chance." He clinched the matter by saying if I failed he could punish me, whereas he couldn't punish one of his officers who failed at a trade not his own.

The next day at roll call, after singing "Cara al Sol," I shouted to the ranks: "I'm going to call out all the trades I need: carpenters, one step forward!" Then we assembled joiners, fitters, mechanics, smiths, masons, etc. I did this for each of the six companies of the battalion. Their names and specialties were written down. Finally with the help of two good officers who wanted to aid me we made index cards for all the skilled workers.

At roll call the following day I told the skilled workers of each company which workshop to go to. From those who had no trade we formed maintenance and cleanup teams. The workshops were dirty. We began by cleaning them and whitewashing the walls. The excavators filled the holes and ruts of the courtyard, cut away the grass growing in the walls of the enclosure and made earthen benches along the walls. There was an empty large hall. We cleaned and whitewashed it: it would be the recreation room where the workers could play cards, chess, checkers and so on. We checked the machines in the workshops and threw the worn-out ones onto the scrap heap. The others we repaired and greased. Each worker was responsible for one machine; he would always be at the same one. The same went for the vises. There were eighteen of them; to each one a set of tools was assigned and the worker was responsible.

I appointed my friend Cortal foreman. After we repaired the workshops he was going to work in the factories in the city. The Catalan was a tailor. I appointed him head of the sewing workshop. A team would recover tarpaulins from the trucks and upholstery from the automobiles. The Catalan and four other tailors were to make gloves, visors, working clothes, towels for cleaning the hands and even sheets for the beds.

The Basque miners, who were strongest as a group, were set to breaking up the scrap metal for melting down. The mechanics were to dismantle the motors; before, everything had simply been smashed and burned with no parts salvaged. The ground was littered with pieces of melted aluminum that had been thrown away as slag. By luck I found five chemists who could teach the others to recognize the various metals by their sound and color.

Soon we were organized. The trucks no longer unloaded just anywhere. Heaps were made by the sheds, each with its own group of mechanics, smashers and sorters; and all around were teams of men, about a hundred of them, carrying the sorted scrap to the workshops. I had all the large cans collected and straps put on them, like the ones grape pickers use. The sorters showed the pieces to an inspector who marked them with chalk. Then the iron, copper, aluminum, tin, lead, etc. were put in separate cans. The large pieces were put on carts I had made with auto wheels. Each transporter was detailed to a can of metal and knew where to take it when it was full. He emptied it at the hearth assigned to that kind of metal, without needing to say each time that this load was iron, this load copper and so on. I got the transporters used to doing their work without haste but going back and forth regularly without stopping.

There was a team of crushers for the boxes, cans and sheets thin enough to be bent. Another team smashed the big pieces with a three-ton ball on a windlass. There were teams for melting wire in cauldrons made from the gas tanks of trucks. The spools of wire melted easily and afterward they were sent to the hearths.

At the end of a fortnight you could begin to see the results of organization. The Maestranza was like an anthill, and production was already four times what it had been before. After forty days I was able to reduce the personnel of the scrap metal works. The trucks unloaded scrap on one side of the workshops and then went to load up ingots on the other, making an organized circuit. I had a canteen set up for the drivers. I noticed there were many Italian trucks; almost all the scrap iron went to Italy. I told myself I was probably stupid to work like that for the Fascists. But I had won my battle.

Now I could pay more attention to the infirmary and the sick again. There were many factories in the city and I made the rounds there every afternoon. Once I was called to the Globo prison camp, the one where we had been formed into a company. There was an epidemic of mange. When they couldn't stop it they asked for *el médico francés*. I went there and had the company taken to the bank of the river Henares. Everyone stripped and washed thoroughly with soap. Afterward each man was smeared with a salve of my own composition: lard and sulphur. Finally they lay in the sun. We repeated the treatment day after day. When the bodies were well peeled, the mange had disappeared and the commandant said to me with a smile, "Another small battle won by the Frenchman!"

I won another amusing one. In going to treat the mange at the Globo camp, I noticed a herd of cows on the riverbank guarded by a soldier. But when the animals went to drink he couldn't watch them all. Often one fell into the water. When a cow falls into the water it drinks through the behind, swells up, can't climb out and drowns.

That gave me an idea. I went to my commandant and told him I had found a way to augment our battalion's meat ration. I recounted the story of the cows at the camp in Globo, and how when one fell in the water even ten or fifteen men couldn't pull it out. But I had worked out a way. We would make a deal: I would pull all the cows out of the water, but those that drowned or had to be slaughtered would be for our company. The commandant said, "Good! Another little battle," and he advised the captain of the detachment guarding the animals.

Four days later they telephoned that five cows and a calf were in the river. I had my material ready and our truck sped off at once like firemen going to a fire. I had five husky Basque miners and the two butchers of the battalion with me. We arrived and quickly unloaded our equipment: two tackles, one with rope, the other with chain. We drove in two mining stakes and made fast the rope and chain. Two cows were already quite swollen, and two others were in water up to their bellies with the calf beside them. I sent two Basques to put a lasso around the cows' necks and we pulled gently with the tackles. The first two came out of the water easily with the calf. But they couldn't walk. The two that were already swollen up only had to be pulled to the bank. There the butchers killed them, emptied them of water and cut them up. Pushing gently, we led the two saved cows to the Globo camp. I left the equipment under the guard of the soldiers. Then we loaded the meat in sacks onto the truck and put the little calf, which was alive and well, inside too.

When we got back to the Maestranza, the two butchers carried the meat to the kitchen. They gave me a big piece of good beefsteak the next day and I had a feast with Cortal and the Catalan. The little calf had a room of his own. Prisoners were detailed to bring him fresh grass and carob beans. After only a few days he was plump. He was as spirited and affectionate as a dog. We called him Blackie.

The two old nursing nuns no longer came to the Maestranza. Cortal and I could handle things alone. The cases that seemed critical I sent to the hospital. But the nuns had asked for a team of masons to make some repairs at the convent. I sent Cortal and his men, and now the convent became part of my morning rounds.

You entered through a large black door with a smaller

one behind it. The nuns were all French. Their habit was black with a sort of white bonnet on their heads. They ran a school in French for the children of the rich townspeople who paid them well. They also went into the town to give French lessons in the Spanish schools. Others went to care for the sick. The mother superior was a very pretty Spaniard. On a visit to the convent I learned that she like myself was from Almería and we quickly became friends.

My team of masons worked in the chapel. Cortal had erected huge scaffoldings and was repairing the vaults. During the war the roof had not been properly looked after and water had seeped in. A painting above the altar had suffered especially, and it was the most precious of all because it was of the patron saint of the convent. I asked the pretty mother superior to permit me to restore it. She agreed with delight. I asked her to get paints, linseed oil and brushes. The next day I set to work. I sized the canvas with egg white, then retouched the places where the paint had fallen off, particularly the lower part where many images had almost disappeared. Then with linseed oil I made the whole canvas shine. It took me many days. At noon they gave me dinner in the kitchen. What a kitchen! Enormous and equipped with everything imaginable. They gave me all the white bread I wanted, with cold meat, fruit and a bottle of good wine. They even gave me tobacco as I had noticed there were sisters who smoked cigarettes in secret. This is the way it often is with nuns who live a good deal outside the convent walls. They were not sad and locked in. I had seen Frenchwomen arriving from France to enter the convent. You could recognize them easily: they were not like the Spanish women with no makeup on their faces. They came with rouge and lipstick. The next day no more, and their hair was shorn.

When I finished the painting, the mother superior in- vited the commandant. He had seen the painting be- fore. He couldn't believe it. He said, "He has won battles for me, and now he produces miracles!" He congratu- lated me over and over. As for myself, what I had done was above all for my comrades, for when I left each day my rucksack was stuffed with sandwiches, bread and meat, and always a bottle of wine.

The mother superior and I became better and better friends. We would go to her office and there she told me stories of my native town and also of her life in France. One morning she had me come to her room. She closed the door. On the table there were wine and cakes. We drank well and suddenly she kissed me and then un- dressed. We got into bed and enjoyed ourselves. When I started to come I wanted to restrain myself, but she pressed me against her and said, "Go ahead, don't be afraid; if anything happens I know where to dispose of it forever." When we finished making love I left and she accompanied me to the gate. After that, each time that I visited the convent I had a bit of everything to eat and drink, and then spent a pleasant hour with pretty Sis- ter Inez.

Blackie, our calf, became more and more handsome and gentle. Each evening a prisoner would take him for a walk around the Maestranza where good grass grew along the wall. One evening when I came back I found the comrades very sad. The lieutenant from Santander had ordered the butcher to slaughter the calf that morning. After he had taken the best morsels, he said the rest was for the company. When I came in and the cook showed me Blackie all in pieces I was grieved. I wasn't the only one. At noon and evening the company refused to eat. They took nothing but bread and a glass of wine.

Condemned

O NE FINE MORNING the time came for our departure. We left with regret; we had been well off at the Maestranza. We had organized ourselves, the output at work was good, we had formed habits and made acquaintances — and now we had to leave Guadalajara to go to Alcalá de Henares.*

The trucks took us to a barracks right in front of the celebrated prison of Alcalá. When we got out, everything was still chaos. There were many barracks in the city. Since the departure of the Republican troops, the Nationalists had occupied many of them. But this one had remained as it had been at the moment of the

---

*Alcalá de Henares is situated fifteen miles northwest of Madrid, at the halfway mark between Guadalajara and the capital. The final battles of the war took place in this area: at the end of March 1938 the Nationalist armies coming from the North and from the direction of Toledo joined forces at Alcalá de Henares. V. G.

Republican retreat. There were even Russian tanks abandoned in the courtyard.

Inside, the situation was the same. The entire company set to work throwing out, cleaning, sweeping, and putting the place back in order. I went around with the Catalan looking for a room for the pharmacy. The soldiers and their officers had taken over the ground floor. The prisoners were on the second in two big halls. At the end of these there were many empty rooms. In one of these, which must have been an office, there were still pigeonholes and files full of papers ranged along the walls. I examined them; they were the archives of the barracks: maps and identity cards with photos of all the soldiers and officers who had been with the Republicans. There were about two thousand. When I saw that, I picked up some of the sacks lying around everywhere and with Cortal and the Catalan, we filled them in haste with all these papers which must not fall into the hands of the Nationalists. Then we took the sacks down to the courtyard. We quickly built a bonfire with old straw mattresses and boards. We emptied the sacks in the middle of the pile and lit it.

When we were sure that all the papers were burned, we went back up. I took the largest room and all three of us settled in. In the afternoon they brought us beds and we spent two days putting everything in order.

The work began. One part of the company was marched to the cathedral. It was on a large square in the center of the city. A large part of the cathedral was in ruins as were quite a few houses around it; the porch of the cathedral and most of the square itself were deep in rubble. The prisoners' first job was to clear the debris from the square. They began by loading it onto trucks, putting the good stones aside in piles. The trucks were emptied in the river Henares at the edge of the city. The banks were well wooded. There were many gardens and licorice groves. Thirty prisoners from my company were already busy digging the licorice roots out with pickaxes. They washed them in the river and spread them out. When they dried, they were put in sacks and sent to Madrid.

I went all around visiting my prisoners, in the city, at the riverbank and at the cathedral. The fifth day, out of curiosity I went into the cathedral, of which the porch was now cleared of debris. On the left there was an opening which seemed to lead underground. You had to bend way over to get through. I slithered in and ended up in a vaulted room whose walls were full of holes; they were crypts for the dead. In one corner, stretched out stiff on the flagstone, was the corpse of a woman. She was about twenty and looked almost as though she were alive. In another corner there was a pile of skeletons, bones and baby skulls no bigger than a fist. In the middle of the room seven corpses lay side by side. They were all dressed differently: three Republican officers, three civilians and a young man in a priest's cassock. I climbed up to the church, made as if I had seen nothing, and went back to the barracks without saying a word. You had to know how to hold your tongue if you wanted to stay alive.

On Sunday we were taken to Mass. All neatly dressed, we marched singing in ranks of three. After dinner, a stew of mutton bones, potatoes, chick-peas, lentils and beans, we were at liberty for the afternoon.

There wasn't much to do in the city. The little money we had usually went for bread. We seldom could buy drinks. Cortal, the Catalan and I explored together. We were happy. I got some bottles of wine, sandwiches and a large loaf of bread in exchange for some cans of milk. Since we couldn't take anything back to the barracks, we ate like pigs. Afterwards we went to a small square where there was a fountain. We sat on the stones and watched the girls and women who came to get water.

One morning the next week we were ordered to dress neatly and we were taken to the church, even though it wasn't Sunday. We were told to sit in the choir. It seemed we were to go to confession. After a while, they called us one by one. We went to the side chapels. A priest was seated in each one. There was a little screen in front of him, and behind it a chair on which one kneeled. My priest was fat and told me to speak loudly as he was hard of hearing. He asked me a lot of foolish questions, with much malice, and I was astonished to see that he had a notebook on a little table by his side in which he wrote something at each of my replies. This seemed more like an interrogation than a confession. I was on my guard right away. He asked me if I had ever gone to see women. I replied, "Yes, from time to time, in the bars." He said, "That is not good. That is a sin." Then he asked me if I had ever stolen. I said, "Yes, when I was a little boy. I took all kinds of fruit in the orchards and tore up birds' nests." He answered, "That is not good. That is a sin." He asked me if I went to church when I was small. Answer: "I made my communion and confessed to the bishop." That time he said that was good, I had been a good boy. Then came the last question: "Did you ever kill anyone during the war, in the interior or at the front?" He added that I must tell the truth, that he would transmit the answer to God. I replied, "During the revolution and the war, I never got involved in politics. I belonged to no organization. At the front I couldn't say whether I had killed anyone. When the other side fired, we fired back, and we didn't have time to see anything, because when we raised our heads the bullets and shells whistled around our ears." He told me, "That's right. For that go to the foot of the altar and say five Hail Marys and ask pardon of Jesus, Francisco." And while I got up he wrote in his notebook.

The next morning we again had to wear our best clothes. They took us to a large building at the side of the church. We were lined up in ranks in a large court-yard. Then, ten by ten, we entered a fine hall when our names were called. Francoist officers were seated at a large table. Civil Guardsmen stood at the side. All ten of us were told to sit on a bench. It was the Francoist military tribunal.

Then an officer of low rank, apparently the judge, picked up a paper. I thought they would interrogate us as they had done at Logroño, but this time there were no cigarettes and the judge didn't even look at us. He spoke with his colleagues and then began to read rapidly from the paper. Such and such, such and such, ten years, such and such, such and such, twenty years, then to me and another, thirty years. The judge said nothing to the two men behind me but the Civil Guardsmen came over and took them away. When I turned my head to see where they were going, I saw the five priests who had interrogated us the previous day seated at the end of the hall. They were sitting in armchairs laughing and talking together. Everything had been quickly expedited. Within an hour of leaving we were on our way back to the barracks. We changed clothes and went back to our usual work. But that evening, at roll call, twenty-eight of our comrades were missing. The next day I learned that they had been shot on the Campo de la Bota in Guadalajara.

A week passed and one day an army doctor from Madrid arrived. He was charged with visiting all the barracks in Alcalá. He was not a doctor; he was a bandit. Mean, drunken, he was always loaded to the gills. When he came to my infirmary he still smelled of anisette. He had a bottle in his medical bag, and in the office I had prepared for him he put in a locked cupboard full of bottles of wine. He prescribed aspirin for all the sick, regardless of what their trouble was. The next day it was a glass of castor oil. So most of the prisoners stopped coming. When they saw me they asked me for medicine. But I received less and less. "So much the better," he told me, "they're all Reds." I said there were soldiers too. He replied they were worth no more than the Reds, they were all illiterate sluggards who could neither maintain discipline nor guard the Reds. One evening he came back from Madrid full of wine. As he got out of his car and crossed the courtyard he began beating the prisoners with his riding crop. After that they hid when they saw him coming, and even if they were keeling over with fever they preferred to say nothing rather than go to him. As a result the doctor angrily ordered punishments for no reason and had all Sunday liberty canceled. In addition to that the food became bad and the commandant no longer came to visit us.

One day we were changing barracks and I happened

to see our provisions arrive. There were quarters of meat, fruits, boxes of milk, sacks of dried vegetables and also fresh vegetables: cabbage, carrots, potatoes and squash. But when the truck left they had put half of the supply back into it.

Shortly after that I was sent to the hospital in Madrid to have a tumor removed. It had appeared behind my ear some time before. I stayed there for a week. The commandant came to visit me. He said the drunken army doctor had been sent to Málaga. That was good news. Then I told the commandant what had happened to the provisions.

One morning after my return the provisions truck arrived and right away the commandant appeared with two Civil Guardsmen, who checked the merchandise. When the vegetable van arrived, the officer of the guard sought to have it leave again without unloading. A dispute arose and a soldier came to inform the commandant. This time he understood. He arrested a captain, a lieutenant, two sergeants and seven soldiers. They were running a black market worth thousands of pesetas. From then on we ate much better.

A week later the company was sent back to Guadalajara, but not to the Maestranza. We found ourselves at the Globo camp, the one where we had been formed into a disciplinary battalion. Things were different there.

The camp was surrounded by barbed wire and there were sentries everywhere. No one could go out except me, as I still had the pass signed by the commanding general. I went to a lot of trouble to smuggle in food and cigarettes. Several battalions were brought together in the camp. I soon became popular with everyone. They knew I was a friend of the commandant, and even the officers of the other battalions came to talk with me. They called me *el francés*. But little by little the atmosphere changed. The company had to work inside the camp at jobs that made no sense. Trucks came in loaded with supplies, we unloaded them, sorted the supplies, and then loaded them again. Others unloaded boards and reloaded boards, and some were set to filling holes with earth and stones. All the while we were badly treated, and there was no liberty on Sundays, even to go to Mass. We were not workers anymore, we were convicts.

And then, little by little, they began putting many comrades on parole. For that you had to be sentenced for not more than twenty years, and to receive a certificate from the Civil Guard, the priest and the mayor of your village. In addition you needed a certificate of good conduct from the commandant of your battalion. I noticed that not many workers were freed. My friend Cortal was liberated; his brother-in-law was a country policeman in the village of his parents near Valencia. They were able to send all the certificates. The Catalan tailor and the Catalan wood merchant were also freed, and two Basques who were good friends of mine. All gave me their addresses; I wrote them down on a block of cigarette papers I carried to make notes of everything of interest in a private code. As there was no writing on the first or last page, no one would suspect it was a notebook with addresses. I had nothing to hope for myself. I had been sentenced to thirty years and had no family in Spain, only the good commandant who still talked to me whenever he came to the hospital and told me to be patient and one day I could live with him and be treated like a son. But in a prison camp there were no battles to be won. Before, we had cared about our work and we had been like a family. All that was over. We went back to thinking of our guards as enemies. We soon found there were spies among us. We caught one of them and strangled him in the toilets. That stirred up the whole camp. A very mean guard had mistreated some prisoners. The next day he was found dead, his neck broken by stone blows. The whole camp was punished then. For two hours in the morning and two more in the afternoon, all the companies drawn up in ranks had to stand with their arm raised singing "Cara al Sol." It was extremely tiring. It went on for three days.

That was not a good way to make us quiet down. The spirit of revolution returned, and we became militant. We appointed two leaders from each company and held meetings at five or six in the evening. One old militant was a radio specialist. We built a receiving set. I gave him small bottles from my pharmacy and with these and bits of wire he succeeded in making radio tubes. With earphones we could easily hear French stations. We organized a news service. On little pieces of paper we would write "The rosebushes are in bloom," meaning there had been a victory. More often the papers were folded a certain way or were punched with holes which made a design when they were unfolded. As I was allowed to come and go, it was my job to carry the notes to the little bar by the road at the entrance to the camp. From there the owner's wife circulated them, as no one had a radio. Some days later they sent me back with packages and even some money for the prisoners. It was funny; we who were locked in informed those who were free.

It went on like this for two months. Some more prisoners were freed; others were taken away to be shot or put in jails. I was now one of the old gang, still popular, still respected. I had nothing to complain of.

Escape

I WASN'T planning to spend thirty years of my life in a prison camp. I studied the map of Spain in secret and casually found out as much as I could from my fellow prisoners about where the railroads and electric lines were, where there were few roads, which mountains were covered with trees, and so on. You had to plan well if you wanted to escape. If you were arrested without papers there was no prison and no trial: they shot you on the spot and you were lucky if they didn't torture you first.

One Thursday afternoon I took a can of milk, went to the bar and traded it for a loaf of bread and a big hunk of red sausage. I filled my canteen with wine and asked the bartender to keep it for me. I would come back for it that night; if the bar was closed he was to leave it on the windowsill. Then I checked the bridge to see whether any Civil Guardsmen were stationed there. They weren't. I went back to camp.

After supper I joked for a while with Sergeant Gil, then went over to the arms depot. The sentinel on duty was a Galician who knew me well. He asked me what I wanted and I told him Sergeant Gil had sent me to make a report on the armament. I said he could come in with me if he liked. He replied he would stay outside to smoke his pipe as that was forbidden inside. I went in and saw four boxes of grenades, three heavy-caliber 7.65 automatics with clips, more than a dozen boxes of bullets and a dagger used as a letter opener. The dagger I stuck in my belt; I put an automatic, four clips and two boxes of bullets in my pockets and stuffed two grenades inside my jacket. Then I picked up a sheet of paper and left calmly after relocking the door. The sentry was still sitting on his rock. He smiled as I walked away.

When I got back to the barracks I put the grenades and ammunition in my rucksack with two cans of milk, some twenty cubes of sugar I'd saved, a bottle of alcohol, four dressings, aspirin and a pair of scissors. On top I packed my towel, soap, flashlight and the block of cigarette paper on which I'd written the addresses of my friends who were still free.

Slinging on the loaded rucksack, I went to the guard post and asked for the officer. I told him I had to go to the hospital for an urgent case. He gave me a pass for the village and I walked out through the main gate of the camp.

The bar was still open. I drank a glass of wine, ate a few olives and took my bundle of food. The bartender's wife gave me another big chunk of bread. By now it was really dark. I crossed the bridge without trouble but on the other side a Civil Guardsman patrol stopped me. I was in uniform: Francoist cap with the red and yellow ball, pants with wooden buttons, belted gray tunic with Red Cross armband, another red cross on my rucksack. Down to my khaki shirt it was all brand-new. One guard examined my pass — signature of the commanding gen-eneral of the Guadalajara region, signature of the officer of the day at the camp. All was in order. They let me pass.

The worst was over. At the edge of town I took the road to the mountains. From there I could follow the left bank of the river; climbing toward its source I would reach Aragón. I walked all night without meeting a liv-ing soul. At dawn I stopped in a clearing deep in the woods, ate a little and slipped into a thicket to rest safe from any surprise.

I didn't know what time it was, or what day, or even exactly what month.* I only knew that it was summer and that I had been a prisoner for two years. Shaded by my thicket from the bright sun, I fell asleep. When I awoke I didn't know how long I had slept. How good it was to be free! How beautiful the flowers, the trees, the singing birds, the sound of the stream running over the pebbles.

At last I started off again, steadily following the river along the mountain paths. At the slightest sound I jumped behind a bush, automatic in hand ready to fire. The outdoors had given me a good appetite and I soon finished my provisions. When the wine was gone I re-

---

*Francisco escaped in July 1940. V. G.

filled my canteen with water from springs. On one mountain I walked through a forest where I found sweet acorns and wild apples and even some arbutus berries. The fruit was good but if you ate too much of it you didn't need a laxative! Drinking water after eating gave me a stomachache. But it was no trouble to attend to the natural necessities and there was fine grass for wiping.

I covered ground with ease, counting the nights to keep track of time. When I awoke at sunrise on the fourth day, I saw four woodcutters coming toward the thicket where I had slept. They carried an ax and a large saw and each had a rucksack on his back. I waited until they had passed and then got up and followed them from a distance. They stopped in a clearing and set to work. I watched and when they finally sat down on the logs to eat breakfast I went up to them. They were surprised to see me but when I asked for something to eat they each gave me some bread, cheese, tomato and red sausage, even a little wine and lots of spring water. They told me I was five kilometers from Sigüenza. When I came out of the forest, the path would lead past a big farm owned by a Falangist leader. There was a Civil Guard post there. He controlled all the surrounding country and had had many people of the region arrested.* The woodcutters advised me to be very careful, and certainly not to ask for anything at the farm. If the master saw me he would have me arrested at once.

I thanked the woodcutters and set off along the path. At the edge of the forest the orchards began. Water

---

*Francisco had come into a region that had been held by the Nationalists since the beginning of the war. V. G.

flowed everywhere. Hidden behind a small wall, I studied the farm. A very pretty farm, large courtyard, women working in the fields, two men with a mule. I slipped into an orchard and began gathering fine apricots, peaches, plums and pears. Farther on I found tomatoes and lettuce. I filled my rucksack and went back to the path. Some two hundred yards from the farm I turned onto the road to Sigüenza. After resting a bit in the shelter of a grove, I hurried on so that I could cross the town before nightfall. I went right down the main street; there were many people about and I would attract less attention that way. Once I was outside the town I left the highway to take a road leading past a quarry where I had worked as a prisoner.

Now I was going into familiar country. As far as La Olmeda and Horna it was just right for me: high mountains with springs everywhere, isolated farms where I could find food, many fruit trees, especially figs and freshly ripe walnuts. I made good time that night along paths lighted by the moon. When morning came I slept hidden among the trees. In the afternoon I went on again, guided now by the railroad track to Zaragoza, my rucksack full with fruits and nuts. I had found a good stone and when I stopped to rest I sharpened my dagger and practiced throwing it at trees. It went like this for three nights. Ah, how good it was to be free! It was cool at this altitude, the going was easy and I could walk or sleep at will without losing sight of the railway.

One morning, just after leaving my thicket, I spied two Civil Guardsmen coming down the path. I sprang behind a rock; here was a chance to try out my 7.65.

They came on, rifles in hand, chatting as they walked. When they were ten yards away I aimed for the heart of the first and fired rapidly at the belly of the other. Both men fell. I ran up and finished off the second; the first was already dead. After taking their lighters, money (380 pesetas) and two brand-new Mausers, I dragged the bodies to a pit and covered them with branches. I went back to the path for their rifles and, finding an old pair of pants a little farther down the path, wrapped up the guns and buried them at the foot of a big pine. Then I went on in the direction of La Olmeda.

Here the mountains were covered with reddish earth. Very few trees; mostly wheatfields and vineyards, from time to time some fruit trees. I traveled cautiously by small stages, resting often. At last I came in view of the mountain village I was looking for. A couple of hundred yards outside it stood an isolated house. I knew the two women who lived there. Often when I was a prisoner they had given me bread and meat in exchange for a can of milk. The husband of one had been shot by the Francoists.

I hid in the rocks until dark, then knocked at the door. The women recognized me and invited me to come in, realizing I had escaped. They were anxious to know whether someone could have seen me come to their house. I said I had met no one. The younger one took a basket saying she would go to the village to get bread from her aunt.

In Spain at that time you couldn't trust civilians. Many were inclined to denounce you in order to assure their own security with the Francoists. I went upstairs to watch the path; the night was moonlit. The old woman brought me peasant clothes and put mine to soak in a big tub. I put my weapons into a cupboard. After a while I saw the young woman coming back down the path with two large loaves. She was alone.

Then they bolted the door and set the table. Good vegetable soup, beans, bread made with good flour, wine. We sat for a bit talking and cracking nuts. Then, sleepy, I went to bed.

In the morning the young woman brought me a big bowl of milk fresh from their two goats to go with the bread and butter. When I went downstairs I found my clothes all clean and drying before the fire. The women said there was nothing to fear, they seldom had visitors. At noon, during dinner, the old one told me of a man sought by the military police who had been hiding for nearly a year in the granary of a house in the village. He had been one of the volunteers in Durruti's column.* If the Civil Guardsmen found him, he would be shot on the spot and the woman hiding him would probably be killed too. She was their cousin.

That interested me. I asked the young woman to take him a message. She was to tell him who I was, that I was trying to escape to France, that I would fight to the death if necessary. If he remained in hiding he would be captured eventually. If he came with me he would have a chance to recover his freedom, and if you had to die it was better to die fighting like a man than to be killed like a rat coming out of a hole. But he would have to decide that evening. I was leaving tomorrow.

---

*Durruti was an anarchist leader; his column fought in Aragón outside Zaragoza, then at Madrid where Durruti was killed. V. G.

The woman took her basket — women never go out without baskets on their arms in this part of the country — and went to the village. When she returned she had a surprise: the man would come that night with another one also sought by the military police.

By evening my clothes were dry. The young woman ironed while the old one mended them. I had her sew deep, narrow bullet pockets around the inside of my jacket and a little pocket for the dagger inside my pants at the hip. I noticed the two women had a well-made switchblade knife with a solid hilt. I remarked it would be very useful to have. They gladly gave it to me.

When night fell the young one went out back to watch for the two men, who were to meet her at the end of the garden. They came in and we shook hands. We sat down at the table and while we ate I told them who I was, what I had done during the war, how I had been a prisoner and escaped. Then I unfolded my plan.

One man alone had little chance of getting across country occupied by the enemy. He could not cover himself from ambush by Civil Guardsmen when he went to fill the canteen at a spring. It was the same when he went up to a farm to ask for food and didn't know whether he would find friends or enemies. And he couldn't attack; and to get through enemies you had to attack without cease. A man who was running away was a dead man. You must always be the hunter, never the rabbit. Only as guerrillas could we make it to the frontier, and for that we had to gather a band, as we were starting to do this evening, from all the Republicans hidden in the villages or mountains who wanted to join us to continue the fight and find liberty or death. But all those who wanted to come along had to obey me. They had to follow the law of the guerrillas: no pity for mercenaries, the Civil Guard or army officers, for if a guerrilla fell into their hands it was torture and death. But the guerrillas must respect women, children and old people, and if they met girls in the mountains they must never touch them — that was sacred. If you had to kill a civilian, it must be because he was a spy, a person who had had others arrested, or a Falangist leader who had brought Republicans to trial and imprisonment. Then it would be his turn to be condemned and punished. But even then only with the accord of all, like a tribunal marked with the great R of the Republic. As for any money found on enemy corpses, I alone would guard it. It would be returned in full to the poor peasants who helped us.

I told them how I had commanded a group of guerrillas in the International Brigade, how I had learned by actual fighting the special tactics of this kind of combat. It was because of my experience that I would give the orders and by following them they would save their own lives and do the most possible damage to the enemy.

Both men agreed. They told me what they had done in the war. Vicente, the younger, medium in build and rather beefy, had served as an artilleryman in the Durruti Column. He didn't say much but listened with eyes moving restlessly around in all directions. The other, Luis, talked on and on using his tobacco-stained hands as much as his mouth. He was a big, quick man and had been, he said, political commissar in Lister's corps. Vicente was an anarchist.

After supper I took them upstairs. Big Luis was surprised by the quality of my arsenal. He ran his fingers along the dagger and admired the way it cut like a razor. Vicente only had an old five-chamber revolver which he said he couldn't use very well. He was good with all other weapons including knife and dagger. But he wasn't good at the revolver. Big Luis was armed with a hunting rifle and two hundred cartridges. It was behind the garden gate with his ammunition belt. He admitted that he too was a bad shot with the revolver.

I explained the orders to them, cries for rallying in case of surprise, cries of attack, cries of command. We talked until one in the morning. They thought we would leave at night, but I decided to take to the mountains in full daylight after dinner. We went to bed and slept till ten.

I got back into my Francoist uniform with the Red Cross armband. Dagger in its pants pocket, knife and grenade in the jacket pockets, another grenade and canteen in new pockets sewn on the rucksack. Then a Mauser and two clips. My rucksack was packed with the pharmacy, bread and sausages.

Vicente and Luis wore dark brown peasant corduroy. Vicente's rucksack contained a can of lard, a large load of bread, three large sausages, a big chunk of dried ham, big box of salt, pepper, a small bottle of vinegar, a bottle of wine, three packages of cigarettes and the tablecloth. He was our cook. In one pocket he had a knife and my Astra automatic with three clips, in the other a grenade, two boxes of bullets, and a good supply of matches, tobacco and cigarettes even though he smoked little. Big Luis had another large loaf, another big chunk of dried ham, some sausages, two chocolate bars, shaving soap, a razor with five blades and two towels. I said no fruit; to protect your movements you had to load yourself down as little as possible. I gave Luis the other Mauser with a full clip and a grenade. He had an ordinary but very large knife. He also had his pockets full of tobacco and cigarettes, and a pipe hung at his belt. On his shoulder was his hunting rifle, at his waist the ammunition belt, and, slung on a bandolier, a two-liter canteen of wine.

When our preparations were finished, we went down to the kitchen. We ate and drank well. We smoked a last cigarette. I gave Vicente's revolver to the old woman telling her to hide it; one day she might have to use it. About three o'clock, going out through the garden, we left for the mountains.

GUERRILLA WARFARE

July, 1940—February, 1941

Dispensing Justice

AFTER NEARLY A YEAR of hiding in a granary, my two men were disoriented by the full daylight of the open countryside. They panicked and wanted to run, which was exactly what we must not do. I held them back and when we found shelter in the mountains after marching two miles I ordered a halt.

I explained that a guerrilla must never run without good reason or travel without resting. On the contrary, and above all in traversing dangerous regions, he must advance slowly, with prudence. In case of alert or ambush a tired guerrilla is often a lost man. His attention flags, his reactions are slower, and if he has to run he is soon winded and drops behind. For the same reason he must also be sure never to load himself too heavily. He must be ready to sacrifice provisions and even weapons to safeguard his freedom of movement. We would march an hour and rest twenty minutes, for if we always hurried then when the enemy came we would be at the end of our strength, we would have to jettison everything, and the enemy, who would be fresh, would hunt us down and kill us like rabbits.

We went on again, following the ridges and looking for sheltered passages. There were few trees and we had to slide from rock to rock. The trails below were dusty.

The least slip would raise a cloud of dust there. When we passed by trees, I had the two men practice throwing the dagger. Luis was very poor at it, but he was patient: throwing a knife isn't learned at the first try. He had the instincts of a hunter; at the slightest sound he caressed his rifle. But I had given the order never to fire at game; that would make too much noise. Young Vicente began to regain confidence. He knew the region well. Not far from the village of Horna, toward which we were headed, there was a hut where mules were sometimes kept. We found it; there was some straw there. We spent our first night. It was so out of the way that we could sleep without keeping watch. Both men were tired; they were out of training, unlike me; I was used to marching and being hungry. We settled down to sleep but Big Luis snored like a boar and I had to awaken him again and again so that he wouldn't alert all the patrols in the region.

At dawn I got them up and led them to a sheepfold some hundred yards from the Horna village square. I had slept there when my company of prisoners had spent some time in the village. It was deserted. The two men waited for me, hidden behind the gate. I left my rucksack and went to the square, where my bakery was. The door was open. I went in and the baker's wife recognized me at once. She was up early because she was still alone; her husband was still in prison. She understood what I had done and why I had come to find her. I asked for news of the village, whether there were police. No, no police. But there was the priest. He was top man in the village and its surrounding countryside and he had established a reign of terror. Those who didn't pay the tithe at his will he had arrested by the Civil Guardsmen who passed through twice a week. He had already had twenty-five people arrested in the village alone, not counting those arrested in the surrounding countryside. He often took part in the arrests himself. And he refused to sign the certificates which would set prisoners free. Because of him the baker's wife, like so many others, could not get her husband released. The mayor, who was the village butcher, could do nothing against the priest.

When she had finished telling me all this, I gave her money to go and buy as much tobacco for me as she could get. It was rationed, but often in the mountain villages people smoked little and the peasants would willingly sell their share. She came back with five packages of tobacco, a box of cigars, three packages of Canary Islands cigarettes and she added her husband's share: two packages of cigarettes and a big cigar. Then she gave me two big loaves of fresh bread and a box of peaches.

I left and saw two old acquaintances in the square. I said hello. At the sheepfold I found my two friends, gave them the bread and put the peaches in my rucksack. I told them I still had something to do in the village and they must wait for me, ready to leave with all the provisions and ready to cover me with gunfire if they saw me come back running.

I returned to the village and found the fine house of the priest. The gate was ajar. I rapped softly three times. He answered tranquilly, opened the door wide and asked what I wanted. I said, "Is there a Mass this morning?" He answered, "At ten o'clock." I said, "I won't be able to come but I would like to confess a sin which is weighing on me." Then he gave me a serious look and invited me to come in. I did. When we were in his study I sank my dagger between his shoulder blades. My other hand was clapped over his mouth and with a single motion I jerked out the dagger and cut his throat. I let him go and he fell. I searched the drawers of the desk and found a bundle of bills which I pocketed. I went to the kitchen to clean the dagger with a dish-cloth and put it back in its sheath. I found a loaf of bread and half a chicken. I wrapped it all in a news-paper, left and calmly recrossed the village. Everyone was about by now and people were going to the fields. I rejoined my friends, who were uneasy about all the activity. I gave them the bread and showed them the money. We counted rapidly: 11,200 pesetas, a small fortune. They asked me what I was going to do with it. I told them, "It is the money of the poor; it will be re-turned to the poor."

We started off across the fields. When we came to the mountains, we skirted the edge of the forest. After a while we came in view of a station in a secluded spot, completely surrounded by the forest. I recognized it. The train from Zaragoza to Madrid stopped there to let off the passengers changing for Soria. At the station there was a Civil Guard post for checking the papers of the passengers who changed trains. We were going to attack the post.

From the hill where we were hidden in the trees I ob-served the station with care. We would come up from behind the building and attack from the front. We would await the arrival of the train from Zaragoza and let the transfer of passengers take place and when the little train for Soria, which we could see waiting in the station, had departed, it would be the moment to attack. I had worked as a prisoner loading trains in this station and I had noticed that when the trains left, the Civil Guardsmen went back into their post to talk or play cards.

We waited an hour. Toward six the train came in. Many soldiers and Civil Guardsmen got out and changed to the little train for Soria. We left our packs at the foot of a big tree and began to descend. When we were about ten yards from the station we hid behind a pile of railroad ties. Three Civil Guardsmen stayed on the platform; two others went back into the post. The train to Madrid left, then ten minutes later the train to Soria pulled out, and the three Civil Guardsmen joined the other two inside. The station was deserted. We waited ten minutes. I gave my orders in a low voice. I would come up from behind and throw a grenade through the window. Immediately they would enter from the front, revolvers in hand, while I covered the window. We did it just that way. After the explosion of the grenade I finished off those who weren't already dead. Vicente went into the post while Luis stopped the two civilian employees who had run out in fright from the office of the post. In the post Vicente collected the weapons. I searched the office but took nothing. I made sure no one was hiding anywhere. Vicente went back to get the packs. I made the two civilian employees go into the guard post. At the sight of the corpses they trembled with fear. I told them we never attacked civilians but only enemies of the Republic. I gave them cigarettes while Vicente searched the bodies. Then we left after we had each shaken hands with the two civilians.

Deliberately we set off along the railroad in the direction of Zaragoza, in full view of the employees of the station who watched us depart. We marched a couple of miles between the rails and then left the railroad and went back into the forest; once we were under cover of the trees we turned around, in the direction of Soria. We were tired. I knew a place where there was a fine cover of tall pines. When we got there we settled down for the night.

First of all we counted up our booty: 3,100 pesetas, six cans of food, five revolvers with their clips and ammunition. We didn't encumber ourselves with rifles, we just put them out of commission by slamming their barrels against the corner of a wall. Following our rule I took charge of the money and added it to the priest's hoard. I put one revolver in my pack and stuck another in my belt. Luis took two revolvers, still keeping his rifle. Vicente took another. Now we were if anything too heavily loaded with arms. Finally there was a blanket for each of us and that was good to have, for in the mountains the nights were getting cold.

The night passed and we stayed there all the next morning to rest. I had some observations to make to my two young companions: they had to learn to fire more quickly. I said to the younger that he must take care not to approach, as he had done, a Civil Guardsman who seemed to be mortally wounded. The man might turn over and in the last seconds of his life shoot the guerrilla coming towards him. If I hadn't finished off the wounded man from the window, Vicente would surely have been killed. To the Catalan I said that when he ordered prisoners to raise their hands, he must make sure that they hold their hands all the way up, because if they only held them at head level they could draw a knife from inside their collar and throw it before you knew it. Then too you must always stay at least four yards from the prisoner and have your back pressed against a tree or a wall. If the prisoner seems to be a friend, you mustn't take your eyes off him before being certain, and you still have to watch his gestures closely and especially his eyes. The eyes always give away a decision to attack.

We set off again in the afternoon, making a long detour through the high mountains. We marched three days and nights, making long halts, for we were too heavily burdened with weapons. But in my opinion we would need these weapons. We were careful not to let ourselves be seen and we kept a good distance from every farm. But in passing from one mountain to another, there was one place where we had to descend to the plain and cross a river. We crossed without incident, the water coming up only to our waists. Then we climbed up the other mountain which unfortunately was less thickly wooded.

In the course of the climb we met two men with their mules gathering wood. They warned us to be on our guard. Four or five very dangerous bandits held the heights, and a troop had come to destroy this band. A company of military police and fifteen Civil Guardsmen guarded the bridges, the crossroads and particularly the paths and the entrances of the villages. After nightfall they fired without warning on anybody out of doors.

We thanked them for the information and gave them tobacco and a thousand pesetas each. They were glad to have it. They had been without work for a long time and they were hungry.

We went on and soon reached the top of the ridge. Here it was bare rock. By luck we came upon a small canyon with trees on both sides. Water flowed. Vicente went up to the source to fill the canteens and Luis shot a fine hare. In this gorge I hoped that the sound would be muffled. We lit a fire to roast our hare. While Luis cooked, Vicente practiced throwing his knife at trees and I stretched out pretending to doze. But I stayed awake and listened with my ear pressed against the rock. Like this you could hear someone walking three hundred yards away.

When the hare was done we ate half of it with the bit of dry bread we had left and drank the last of the wine. Afterwards I gathered dead wood and made a large fire. When it was burning high I cut a green branch and threw it on, adding some fresh weeds. A cloud of smoke rose above the trees of the gorge. Then I gave the order for all to hide twenty yards higher up.

We waited two or three hours without moving, speaking or smoking. Then, up the gorge came two men dressed in Republican uniforms. Each had a rifle and a grenade at his belt. They were dirty and bearded, and one carried a blanket on a bandolier. They picked up the hare's skin and threw it away with an angry gesture. Both were uneasy; they looked to the right and the left, ahead and to the rear. Then they advanced toward our position with their rifles still hanging on their shoulders. They stopped when one noticed where I had cut the branch and looked around again on all sides. I watched their movements. Then three more men appeared. The first was dressed like a peasant and wore rope-soled sandals. He had a submachine gun in his arms and two grenades hung at his belt. The other two were dressed half civilian, half military. One had only a pistol in his hand, the other nothing. All three were bearded and their clothes were very dirty. They had nothing on their heads. They marched side by side. Then I gave the signal and we sprang onto the path yelling *"Mano arriba!"* Hands up! They were surprised. The one dressed like a peasant, who must have been the leader, pointed his tommy gun. But I had time to push aside the barrel and already my dagger was against his belly. Some bullets flew. I shouted, "Don't fire, we're Republicans!" Then the leader lowered his tommy gun while Luis and Vicente held the others in check. The leader said they were also former Republican soldiers; they intended to hold the mountain until the Nationalists came. They preferred to die fighting rather than give themselves up to the Fascists who would certainly shoot them.

Then we all embraced and we led them to our cache. They were astonished at our armament. I gave the one who had no weapon a Mauser with two clips. Vicente offered a revolver and the Catalan likewise. I threw in a revolver from my pack. Now we were friends. The leader told me his men were good marchers and that three were particularly good shots. They gave me their names, told of their families and their tribulations.

But we couldn't delay long. The leader thought that the Civil Guard would attack soon because one of their band had been taken prisoner when he went to the village to look for food.

We left and after a while arrived at their hideaway.

175

It was a cave high on the mountain. They had little fresh food but did have some in cans. Their bread was hard as rock, their meat a wild boar nearly whole. Night fell. Then, seated on chunks of wood, we ate sharing all that we had. They were especially glad to get some tobacco. We smoked and talked.

I explained my project: to get back to France. I also explained my tactics: never flee but on the contrary keep attacking, changing directions often in order to deceive and distract the enemy. Never talk at night when you were on the march as the voice carries far then, never smoke at night as a lighted cigarette furnishes a good target for an enemy rifle. I told them of the calls of command; how each man in turn stands guard in a tree when we halt; and all the rules to observe in dealings with the people.

After some hesitation, their leader, who was older than I and who had also been a lieutenant in the army, said that I should have command. So now we were a united band of eight men: myself; their leader Pepe Valero who had given over the command to me; Luis the Catalan, who with one of the new men, Antonio, would look after the cooking; Vicente and another new one, Manuel, who would be responsible for arms captured from the enemy. The two remaining, Enrique and Sánchez, would be our orderlies. During an attack, Enrique would be at my side ready to communicate my orders and Sánchez would stay by Lieutenant Valero. I decided that we would practice maneuvers together as we marched so as to form a troop well trained in the special combat tactics of the guerrilla.

In the morning we divided everything we had so that

each would carry the same load. That meant only about ten or twelve pounds per man, excluding weapons. We had three submachine guns, eight automatics with their clips, nine grenades, two hundred seventy-four bullets and five machine-gun clips. For provisions we had twenty-eight cans of food, a little dried ham, four large sausages and several small ones, some pieces of braised wild boar and eleven boxes of biscuits hard as rocks.

I decided that we must retrace our path and rejoin the railroad to Zaragoza. We walked single file. Valero, who knew these mountains like his own mother, marched at the head. From time to time we practiced maneuvers together: attacking head-on, encircling, dodging, attacking on two sides, attacking with rapid changes of position, coming to the aid of another when called, attacking from two different points and coming together to take cover. It went like this for three days and three nights.

Our provisions now exhausted, we came down to the plain again. We found a large, rather isolated farm. I watched the comings and goings for a good hour. There didn't seem to be any police. Then I sent ahead Vicente and Manuel, who were dressed as peasants. Enrique and I followed at a distance. When we came to the farm they went straight in while we looked around behind the buildings. The other four stayed on the mountainside; posted on a big rock, they could see everything and in case of danger they were to run down and cover us.

Vicente and Manuel were within twenty yards of the entrance to the farm. As soon as Enrique and I reached our position on the side, I shouted the order to attack.

Vicente ran ahead, knocked at the door and jumped to
one side. An old man came out. Automatic in hand,
Manuel went up to him and asked if there were police
inside. He said "No, only the family." Then Vicente
charged in. When I came in with Enrique everyone was
lined up against the wall. A small boy about twelve
years old began to cry. I patted him, said there was
nothing to be afraid of, and gave him a hundred pesetas.
Then the head of the family said, "How many men do
you need food for?" I said, "Fifteen." He gave me the
whole week's bread, five large loaves. Then a ham,
morcilla sausages, some blood sausages, and a big
piece of salt pork. He filled our canteens with wine. A
pair went out to the garden and gathered a basketful of
tomatoes, onions, peppers, eggplants, and apples. The
women made us four large ham sandwiches and served
us four large glasses of wine. From time to time I went
out to have a look around. When everything was ready,
I kissed the little girl, then the little boy who had stopped
crying and who was following me around the house holding my hand. I gave the father a thousand pesetas. He
did not want to take it. I told him paying was the rule of
guerrillas and asked him to forgive us for frightening
them. Then we left loaded like donkeys, but not together:
two of us went out one door, two out the other. When
we joined our companions they were wild with joy. We
sat down at once and began to eat. When we had finished, we divided up the food among the packs. Then
we hung the basket and the two empty bags on a branch
so the peasants would have them back. The Catalan left
a note in the basket: *Thanks. Long live the Republic!*
The second day by a rare chance we saw a column of

armed and laden soldiers climbing up the mountain single file. We were still following the ridges. At nightfall I forbade making a fire or saying the slightest word. We had to speak with gestures and even light our cigarettes under cover. The next day we came in view of the railroad station we had attacked. From the top of the mountain we could see that it was full of soldiers, police and Civil Guardsmen. We continued on, always keeping to the ridges. In the afternoon we again saw soldiers marching single file. They carried automatic rifles and small mortars. They were on maneuver for they were talking, laughing and singing as they marched. Hidden in a thicket, we stopped to observe them. They passed thirty yards from our hiding place. There were too many of them for us to attack; besides, they were soldiers, and we did not seek to kill the sons of the people enlisted by force in the army.

We remained hidden until evening. When night fell we climbed down, crossed a small river and the railroad to Zaragoza and climbed up another mountain. At the top we stopped for the night.

Now our provisions were exhausted again, so we could move along more easily, carrying only our weapons. Wild fruit was plentiful. We marched on for two days. Then we came in sight of a village surrounded by isolated farms. A path descended to one of them. We followed it and all at once there appeared a woman leading a child by one hand and a goat on a leash by the other. In order not to frighten them we walked up slowly. All of us had guns slung from our shoulders. I marched in the lead, my hands in my pockets. When she saw us she stopped dead, not knowing whether to go forward or backward. The child hid in her skirts. Then I stepped forward and asked whether the village had a bakery, a grocery and a tobacco counter. She replied there was a store which sold bread and everything else. She understood who we were and offered to take us to her house which lay behind a large farm; from there we could go to the store. I asked if there was a Civil Guard post in the village. She said no, once a month a patrol came through. The post was in another village on the other side of the mountain. The people of the village were all peasants. She lived with her grandparents and helped them tend the fields. I asked where her husband was. She said, "In France." Then I was reassured.

Still talking, we came to the house. She took us in through the garden and the old ones showed their pleasure at seeing us. They brought us food and drink; then the young woman showed us the granary where we could all sleep.

In the evening, with Enrique and Luis I went out with the young woman. She led us to the store. It was closed; she knocked and called, and a tall, heavy man came out. She spoke to him without fear: these men are Republicans, they want to buy food. The man took us into a large kitchen. Two men having supper offered us wine. My two companions stayed with them to talk about the war while the big one showed me the store, stocked with everything imaginable. I chose eight large loaves of bread, chorizo sausage, cans of tuna and sardines, beans, meat, lard, matches, ten packs of tobacco and ten packages of cigarettes and a large box of cigars. He threw in five packages of cigarettes and some extra cigars. He wrapped everything, added up the bill and led me back to the kitchen. The others were drinking and smoking, and — a rare thing — all laughing together. I paid up, rounding off the bill to two thousand pesetas. The big one was pleased. He returned to the shop and came back with a box of chocolate, three cans of milk, a sack of chick-peas, another of rice and a big carton filled with pots of honey. I told him I couldn't carry so much. He replied, "After supper I'll close the shop and we'll all come up to the farm and spend the evening together."

We waited, talking all around, while they finished supper; then we left by the main street, heavily loaded down. We came to the farmhouse. What a surprise! It was full of women and children. All the village was curious to see us and everyone wanted to know about the war and the situation of the country. I profited from the occasion by asking for a barber. He appeared right away and began to trim and shave the whole troop. Only Lieutenant Valero wanted to keep his beard; as for mine, it was only fuzz anyway. When they had been shaved and barbered, I sent my men to bed. Valero, Vicente and I remained awhile to talk further with the people of the village. They were so excited that we stayed up quite late.

When we finally went to the granary to sleep, I awakened Antonio and Sánchez to stand guard, one at the window and the other in the garden in the rear. There might be Fascists in the village. Better to keep watch than have an unpleasant surprise.

The woman came at dawn to wake us bringing bowls of milk and bread. We divided up the purchases of the previous night and left with regret after such a warm

welcome. The woman and child accompanied us to the
end of the path. She told us how we could reach the
other village beyond the mountain; then she left after
kissing us all, and her little girl did the same.

We set off loaded like donkeys. But we had all the
tobacco we wanted and we smoked like Turks. We
marched a few miles in the direction of the next village
and then, following our custom, turned away towards
the railroad. We followed it at some distance for two
days. Occasionally we saw peasant carts, but each time
we hid and let them pass. If they saw us, we went up to
them openly and asked the way to a town different from
the one we were actually headed towards. We gave the
appearance of following their directions, but after a few
miles we took up our own route again, sometimes even
going over to another mountain. You always had to be
suspicious of the peasants. They lived in fear, and fear
makes you talk.

One morning we came in view of a large village. A
rather good road ran through it, crossing a small river by
a bridge. I stopped awhile watching the traffic. Cars
passed often, and carts, and many people were moving
about their business, crossing and recrossing the river.
To get to the next mountain we had to cross the bridge
where two Civil Guardsmen were stationed to check
people's papers.

We came calmly down to the village. I was in front
with the lieutenant. With his peasant clothing and his
beard he seemed harmless. Still dressed in my uniform,
I looked like a soldier on leave. Our companions followed at a distance. We strolled onto the bridge. When
we came to the two Civil Guardsmen, we pulled out our

automatics and killed them. Our companions ran up at once. Vicente and Manuel did their job while I searched the bodies. We got 410 pesetas, two guns and ammunition, two light rifles, four Lafite grenades and a can of food. We went around the mountain and marched without halt to get a good distance away. We found a dense forest and rested through the rest of the day and the night.

In the morning we were awakened by shouts. The forest was swarming with Civil Guardsmen, military police and even peasants armed with rifles. We applied our tactics: they were coming up, we would go down toward them rather than run away from them. We would cross to a mountain on the other side of the valley. It had no trees, only large rocks. Our pursuers would believe we were continuing under the cover of the trees, without thinking of the bare mountain opposite.

We sneaked cautiously from tree to tree. At the crossing of two paths we spied a band of four men armed with rifles led by a civilian armed with a tommy gun. He was saying in a loud voice, "The bandits are cornered, we've got them." He was in such a hurry he didn't think to guard his flanks. At the moment he appeared before us, our three tommy guns fired in unison. The man with the tommy gun fell stiff as a board. The others were twisted on the ground like empty clothes. We kept on, always very carefully, from tree to tree. Ten minutes later three Civil Guardsmen appeared on our path some distance away. They were running towards us. I signaled to let them approach without firing. When they were at the right distance I threw a grenade. They fell and my companions finished them off on the ground.

We continued on while Vicente and Manuel picked up their tommy guns, discharged their revolvers, took their ammunition and threw their rifles into the bushes. They rejoined us. We hadn't gone twenty yards when a Civil Guardsman on horseback appeared down the path. As soon as he came in range we opened fire; he fell. But he had had time to fire a shot from his revolver. The bullet struck Sánchez in the right shoulder. We couldn't stop to attend to him. There were still men shouting not far from us. We continued on while our wounded one courageously kept the bullet hole closed with his fingers to stanch the flowing blood.

At last we reached the rocky mountain. We clambered up, going from rock to rock, crouching to observe again and again whether the mountain was free of enemies. Finally we came to the top. We were at the end of our strength. There was no noise now. On the other side we rested in the shelter of some large rocks. Vicente and Enrique had helped the wounded Sánchez during our climb. Now I became a medic again. I dispensed ether, then probed for the bullet with my pointed scissors and took it out. I bathed the wound with alcohol and made a square dressing held on with adhesive plaster. Fortunately we hadn't lost any of our provisions. We restored ourselves by eating and drinking, then rested several hours. Valero watched over our wounded companion, who had a fever; each of us stood guard in turn. By morning Sánchez had had a good sleep. He was fit; we were well-rested. We set off in the direction of another forest. In the afternoon I changed the dressing. The wound looked clean and Sánchez marched well, ate with good appetite and enjoyed smoking. Those were good signs.

We came to the forest. We found a well-hidden cave. There was a spring nearby and when we had drunk our fill we went into the cave. The entrance was narrow but after ten yards we came out in a fine grotto so large you would have thought it an old quarry. It was dark. Drops of water fell from the vault. With a tin can, oil and a lighter wick we made a lamp. I went out to see if the light could be perceived: not a glimmer. We made pallets from leafy branches. We passed a good night and felt so comfortable that we decided to stay another night.

We left at dawn. We marched three hours and at the end of the forest we saw a well-cultivated hillside before us. But to get to it we would have to descend into the valley and follow a gorge with a road running through it that must lead to the village. We went down. At the bottom I quickly looked for a less exposed place. A small path left the road in the direction of the top of the hillside. We took it. We had almost reached the top when bullets began to fly from the ridge. We had fallen into an ambush.

We were in the open. In a case like that you must never retreat. A troop in the open in front of a hidden enemy is bound to be wiped out if it tries to run away without being able to entrench itself. I shouted the order to advance straight ahead. That way we could gain the shelter of a small wall bordering the field which separated us from the enemy. There was continued firing of rifles and automatics. From the shelter of the wall I looked around. They were on the edge of an olive grove that extended to the crest. They had neither a machine gun nor a mortar, nor even grenades: we were hardly thirty yards away, they would surely have used them already. But they were numerous. We would attack with grenades, all together but from different positions spaced ten yards apart. Bullets flew over our heads. We had to act fast as the noise of the fusillade would bring reinforcements. We crept to our positions. Two of my men were missing, doubtless hit in the first volleys.

I shouted to attack. We rose up running straight toward the olive grove. They were firing, but our grenades exploded among them, and when we reached them we fired tommy guns one burst at a time to conserve ammunition. They were military police. After ten minutes of combat the firing stopped. All were on the ground except three we had as prisoners. Quickly I counted twenty-seven dead. On our side, Lieutenant Valero, Manuel and Luis the Catalan had been killed. Sánchez, our wounded one, had taken a bullet in the head and several in the belly. He was in agony and I had to finish him with a bullet. Vicente, now alone for the job, collected ammunition for our tommy guns and automatics while I searched the rucksacks of the enemy. Enrique guarded the prisoners and Antonio, stationed below, watched the road. I found only a few cans of food, but in the pocket of one of the policemen there was a large wad of bills. The most precious booty was a brand-new pair of binoculars I could make good use of. I took the Catalan's canteen and without further delay we set off along the ridge of the hill. Then we had to descend again to the plain. There were fields of grain and meadows bordered by trees. We advanced in their shadow. With my binoculars I surveyed the surroundings. My comrades were very sad to have lost their companions. I consoled them as best I could. In war you must never look behind, always ahead. We were well armed: a tommy gun, two automatics and a grenade apiece. We had three loaves of bread and as much water as we wanted from the irrigation canals. As for money, our war treasure now stood at 37,850 pesetas.

As I could now see long distances thanks to the binoculars, I stopped to observe a large village. It had an important railroad station, a junction from which two tracks parted. I recognized the branch line where passengers left the Madrid-Zaragoza line to get on the one heading south in the direction of Valencia. I think the village was named Alcuneza.

I thought over the situation. My men were no longer the same: fear had come over them again since the death of their comrades. We were now only four, not enough to attack, set up ambushes, operate in group maneuvers, or to guard ourselves when traversing a region where we were being hunted. I had kept the prisoners to make them talk. In combat the Civil Guardsman is brave, but as a prisoner he is just a coward; he will talk easily. I knew now that all the police were searching for the gang of a bandit whom they called El Mexicano because of his yell at the moment of attack. So I decided to change sectors. We would go by the quickest routes to Valencia, that is to say even further into conquered territory, some hundred and twenty miles. There I hoped to meet up again with my friend Cortal. He would come back to France with us, bringing along others who like us wanted to regain freedom. I said nothing yet of my plan. Right now we had to execute our prisoners. That hurt me this time because one was only a boy. But they wouldn't hesitate to liquidate us, and that only after having tortured us. We at least struck them down by surprise.

We went around the large village and came to a main

route, the road to Valencia. We followed the road openly. You always had to go where they wouldn't be looking for you. Vicente had regained his confidence, but Antonio was still always at my heels like a scared little dog. We encountered many people, even unarmed soldiers, doubtless on leave. They passed without saying anything but often I read in their eyes what they thought.

We walked several miles and then when no one else was visible on the road we headed into the fields. We crossed through orchards and came across an abandoned cabin. We could rest inside while watching the road through the open door. It was then that I explained my plan. The countryside of Valencia is easier: no mountains, but lots of orchards, tilled fields and rice-fields where we could march well-hidden while still having food. And then too we would have friends.

Before I'd finished speaking some Civil Guardsmen on horseback appeared on the road, looking all around. We went out of the cabin, leaving our packs inside, and hid in some thick brambles. The Civil Guardsmen on the road were getting farther away. But two of them dropped behind to patrol the fields. They passed near us. One of them said, "Maybe they were the men of El Mexicano's band; we'd better search the cabin." They halted their horses twenty yards from the door, advanced rifle in hand and hit the door. One went in; the other remained outside. Vicente and I approached the horses. We let them loose and at the moment the Civil Guardsman came out we fired a volley. They both fell, but one of them had time to fire a shot. The bullet went through my cap.

We dragged the bodies inside. We undressed them

and Antonio and Enrique put on their uniforms. They carried their guns with an extra automatic at the belt and a grenade in the pocket. They marched on either side of Vicente, who was dressed as a peasant, as though they had arrested him. I, still in my Francoist uniform, would walk calmly at a distance like a soldier on a trip. We left our packs, blankets and even our provisions in the cabin. I kept only the binoculars, a roll of gauze with a small bottle of alcohol, some cigars and cigarettes, and of course all our money, 41,220 pesetas. The tommy guns and their ammunition were buried in a thicket. I had my Mauser with five clips and a grenade hidden inside my jacket.

Then we went back to the highway and stood calmly waiting for the bus.

Valencia

A BUS for Mondova stopped. We got on. With our dirty clothes and our beards we must have looked threatening; the passengers seemed uneasy when they saw us. We each paid for a ticket for Mondova. My two false Civil Guardsmen played their part well: they demanded the papers of the passengers.

I went to the back and sat down beside an old lady.

In a short time tongues began to loosen a bit. The old lady said, "Civil Guardsmen with beards like those! Don't they have a barber in their barracks?" I replied they must have been in the mountains looking for bandits. She said in a low voice, "The Civil Guardsmen are often worse bandits than the bandits themselves, and those two sure look it! The newspaper says that the band of El Mexicano attacks farms in the mountains, raping the women and killing the old people and children. . . . *No lo creo, porque estos bandidos tienen padres et madres, como todo el mundo. Es mentira.*" (I don't believe them, because these bandits have fathers and mothers like everyone else. It's a lie). I replied, "*Muchas gracias!*" She looked at me with a smile and pulled out the newspaper. "Look at that. Those aren't women and children." There was a picture showing two Civil Guardsmen hung up by the feet with the caption: TWO MORE VICTIMS OF EL MEXICANO. The old lady seemed quite pleased by it.

The picture was of course a scene staged by the police. I had never had the time or even the notion to hang up the men I had had to execute.

We had been riding about two hours when the bus stopped by a military car. It had had a breakdown and the two officers, a colonel and a Carlist commandant, got onto the bus.

A little before the next town the road passed through mountains barren except for a few shrubs and tufts of esparto grass (feather grass), which was gathered to make rope. I made a sign to my two Civil Guardsmen sitting up front. They had the bus stopped. I got up, saying, "This is where I get off." As I passed Antonio I told him to make the two officers get off. He went to get them. They protested vigorously, especially the major, who said he would file a complaint. He even tried to draw his gun, but Enrique took it. The people on the bus laughed, saying, "If you want to complain, go do it at your barracks." As soon as the officers were outside they waved their arms and shouted. We pushed them into a field while the bus pulled away. Then I said to the colonel, "How many men have you condemned to death in your region?" And to the commandant, "How many Republicans have you thrown in prison all over?" Then the commandant cried "It's El Mexicano!" I executed him and Vicente shot the colonel.

The mountains began three hundred yards from the road. We climbed rapidly to the top. There we were at ease and we advanced calmly around the town of Mondova. From above we saw vans of military police setting out on the road and Civil Guard patrols leaving the town. We advanced slowly as I had to survey all sides with my binoculars. I saw a column of soldiers mounting the trail behind us. They were looking for us on this mountain. We quickly climbed down, crossed the road and went up a small mountain on the other side. There was a large marble quarry on the slope. Trucks came and went from it. Some twenty men were at work. We climbed higher. The mountain was full of pits. We took advantage of them to hide and rest a moment. We kept on and night fell. There was bright moonlight; we marched with ease. We came to a large mountain whose slopes were covered with esparto grass. Here and there were huts made of branches. The esparto grass collectors used them to rest in and to eat their dinner. There were heaps of the hemp piled around.

In the morning the mountain was full of workers. We

had to pass through them. Each worker carried a staff; he twisted the grass around it and then pulled out the tufts with both hands. We talked to them. They were miserable, badly paid. They told us that at the village of Pinoso everyone was searched and had to show his pass. They said there was a canteen a little farther down where you could eat, and even a large shed where you could sleep. I asked two workers to go buy me six loaves of bread, red sausages, cheese and a gourd of wine. I gave them a thousand pesetas. They were dazzled. They had never seen so much money at one time. I told them to say nothing; we would wait for them here. They went off; I followed them through the binoculars. When they went into the canteen, we went down the path and posted ourselves behind a stack of boxes of esparto grass. We waited an hour; no one came out of the canteen. We waited another hour. Another still. Then we went down, making a detour and coming up just behind a shed. From there I could see two Civil Guardsmen standing in front of the door of the canteen. Then I saw one of the men we'd sent with the money for the provisions come out. He laughed, walked a few steps, pissed against a tree, and came on in the direction of the shed. He turned the corner and found himself standing in front of Antonio and Enrique, my two Civil Guardsmen. He recognized them, turned and started to run back toward the canteen. My knife was ready and he fell by the door. At that moment the two Civil Guardsmen, hearing his cries, came out and were killed before they could raise their guns. We went in; Vicente jumped behind the counter and held everyone in place with two revolvers. There were eleven men at the tables. He made them stand and line up against the wall. Then Vicente went into the kitchen: there were two women and two men, one of them a big one, apparently the owner. The other tried to hide behind some empty boxes. Vicente recognized him; it was the other worker, who was supposed to bring our provisions. He killed him in front of everybody. Vicente searched him and found five hundred pesetas in bills of one hundred. I stayed by the door where I could watch for workers coming. I let them enter and told them to stand against the wall, and that they need not be afraid. The big owner gave us a large bag filled with manchego cheese, three large loaves of bread, some blood sausages with onion, two or three pounds of red sausages and four bottles of wine. I gave the owner five hundred pesetas. Then I gave each of the workers and the two women a hundred-peseta note. I told them the two workers we had killed were traitors who had not kept their word. Meanwhile Vicente had searched the bodies of the Civil Guardsmen. He brought me their money; I counted 645 pesetas and tossed it onto the table. I told them to eat and drink well with the money of criminals; then we left in haste. Behind us the workers cried, *"Buena suerte, El Mexicano! Viva la República!"*

We climbed back up the mountain and when we were out of sight of the esparto grass gatherers I started down again along a path that brought us in view of the town of Pinoso. I had the address of a family there. I sent Vicente, who was still dressed in peasant clothes, to ask for directions to their house. We were lucky; it was right at the end of the path, in the quarter of the village where the houses are caves in the mountainside. I went there and found the aunt of my friends. The family itself lived in the village in a regular house. Inside, her cave was like a house with a fireplace and bedrooms, and very clean. Her husband had been shot by the Republicans because he was a Fascist. The Republicans had made her son take all the statues of the saints out of the church and throw them in the fire, along with the benches and the wood of the altar; throughout the war he had been imprisoned and mistreated. When the Francoists entered the village he was very happy to be set free. He presented himself to the new mayor, also secretary of the Falange. He was arrested and shot for what he had done to the church, along with thirty other inhabitants of the village. She told me all that, crying all the time; she suffered so much from feeling all alone. When night came I went to get my three friends and we stayed there resting three days without going out.

The wife of my friend came to see us. Her husband Antonio had escaped into France with the retreating Republicans. She worked as a cleaning woman for a commandant of the Fascist army. She was barely able to support her mother and her father-in-law, who were very old. The woman took our clothes and brought them back the next day neatly washed and ironed. These poor people had little to eat, only large carrots. I inquired about the crops in the surroundings. There were fields of carrots, sweet potatoes, apple orchards, and fields of corn beginning to ripen. But everything was guarded by a very mean field patrol.

That evening we left with our two Civil Guardsmen. We took along two sacks; soon we had them filled with white, red and violet carrots, ears of corn, apples, sweet potatoes and pumpkins. We returned by way of the mountain. In a cabin we found a fine white goat; we took it too. We were back just before sunrise. We lit the fire and all ate together with good appetite. Everything was good, even without bread and wine. After that we slept in a cave; it was cold but we had enough blankets. We stayed eleven days to rest up, never going out in the daytime. No one would dream that the old Catholic aunt had men hiding with her.

We were all rested; it was time to think of leaving. It was Sunday and we were going to leave that night. In the evening I went down to the town. On the square there was a restaurant-café almost across from the mayor's house. I went into the café and sat drinking a vermouth. At last the mayor came in with two of his friends. They drank two or three rounds, laughing and talking. Then they left. In the middle of the square they separated. The mayor turned towards his house. It was dark and there was no moonlight on this side. I followed him and when he was in front of his door I called to him. He turned, I approached and he asked what I wanted in a nasty voice. I replied, "Justice," and planted my dagger in his heart. He fell with only a muffled cry. Rapidly I went up the next street, turned a couple of times and found myself back at the mountain. I came back to the cave and told my friends to go to sleep, we would leave the next day. The old aunt was glad to keep us another day. In the morning Antonio's wife came to bring us the news: the mayor had been found dying in front of his house, killed by a soldier who had fled into the mountains, where the Civil Guardsmen were looking for him. As the woman worked for the

commandant, she had all the news. Civil Guard reinforcements had arrived and were guarding all the routes
to the town. We stayed four more days without going
out, then we left in the evening.

We went over the mountain, and at sunrise came
down on the right. We waited a bit. A truck appeared;
it was empty and going to Valencia. Antonio and Enrique, still dressed as Civil Guardsmen, got in back with
Vicente as their prisoner. I sat beside the driver. We
rolled along. At a bridge two Civil Guardsmen stopped
the truck. When they saw my two Civil Guardsmen with
their prisoner they waved us on.

Now we were coming to the goal of our trip, the town
of Sueca, thirteen miles from Valencia. I had the truck
stop and gave the driver five hundred pesetas. He was
very pleased. Around us were only rice fields and orchards. We met an old peasant; I asked where the grain
mill was. It was a half mile ahead at the side of the
road. There was a small bridge across the canal, the old
mill and behind it a large barn and a small house. There
was nothing but rice fields as far as you could see. I
asked a woman about José Cortal, an escaped prisoner
like myself whose brother-in-law was a country policeman. She called to the house; Cortal came out and ran
towards me. We went in; I could see at a glance they
were very poor. Cortal had had only an occasional few
days' work and had three children to feed. After drinking a glass of wine and talking, I took him aside and explained I had come looking for him to take him to
France. That pleased him right off. In the evening his
brother-in-law, the country policeman, came. When
Cortal told him why I had come, he said not to do that,

that Cortal wasn't like us, he was free and had kept his freedom, but if he was caught with us, we could do nothing to save him; that he, the country policeman, had sent Cortal's certificates, he would lose his job — and a lot more bad advice but all given with goodwill. There it was, I had made the journey for nothing. In one sense he was right; it was I who had deceived myself. We were fighting for our liberty and our lives. Cortal had already found that. He was no longer afire as we were; and I could see he feared capture.

He gave us the little food he had and we ate with good cheer anyway. They wanted us to stay and rest. They would lodge us at the mill. It was in bad shape but the roof was still sound. By day we could stay in the country policeman's house. The next day, at night, my three friends and I took some sacks and two baskets and went foraging. We found a large garden with potatoes and all sorts of vegetables. We returned to the house laden like donkeys and emptied our sacks in Cortal's room. We loaded up again, and on the third trip we went to the rice fields. The rice had been formed into sheaves. We put a sheaf in a sack, stepped on it and the grain came off and filled the baskets. We did this till dawn; during the night we had gathered over a hundred pounds of rice.

When the country policeman saw that the next day, he said nothing. He even seemed glad. He was surprised we had seen no one as there were patrols of Civil Guardsmen who fired without warning at thieves. He had already found eight dead in the field. We ate well but there was still no meat. Close to town there was a large farm where they raised hogs, chickens and rabbits. That evening we made our preparations: we had found a good mule. We put two saddle baskets on him and threw in a couple of large sacks. Then we set out on the road. The night was black and our two Civil Guardsmen marched ahead. Behind, Vicente in peasant dress led the mule. It was completely dark when we arrived. We waited awhile. Through the windows we could see everyone about to sit down to supper. Then my two Civil Guardsmen knocked at the door and went in. Everyone was astonished and remained at the table. But when they saw me enter with Vicente, they understood. One wanted to make trouble. Vicente saw him pick up a butcher knife and shot him in the arm. We let him sit down and I made him a dressing myself with a napkin. Then I spoke to the master. We meant nothing bad, we only wanted some provisions for a band of escaped prisoners. Then the owner and his wife led us to the barn. They had two peasants help us fill the saddle baskets with hams, sausages, lard, salt pork and even two fine dried hams hanging in the fireplace. In the sacks we put chickens, ducks, fourteen fine rabbits, a goose and two turkeys. We tied the sacks onto the baskets and took seven large loaves of bread and all the tobacco we could find. Then after we had drunk a good slug of wine I apologized for the man's wound and counted out four thousand pesetas on the table. We returned by the path through the rice fields. We unloaded and I took the mule back to its owner. I gave him five hundred pesetas. We feasted and drank all night. Cortal and his family were overjoyed. But fear prevented the country policeman from eating well.

The next day the news had spread all through the town. The Civil Guardsmen searched everywhere. They even came to the country policeman to ask him if he had seen anything. We stayed hidden in the mill for ten days, then we left, leaving provisions for many months with Cortal.

We were fresh; we marched all night. By morning we came to the sea and we went along the coast. Fishermen landed on a beach with their catch. They sold us some and soon we were grilling sardines and mackerel. About nine o'clock we reached the suburbs of Valencia. The streets were full. There were many soldiers walking about. We were all clean and carried little; our guns were hidden in our jackets. We strolled along with everyone else.

I went to visit a former fellow prisoner who had given me his address in Valencia. He was the middleweight boxing champion of Spain. He was called El Grande. He had made me a map of the city and I had no trouble finding a dancehall in the Plaza de General Mola where they would know his address. They gave it to me. We went to the apartment building. The concierge said he lived on the fifth floor. I went up alone. I was received by the father, mother and brother of my friend. He worked at the railroad station and wouldn't be back until evening. I asked if I might wait for him. They knew all that I had done for their son and said their house was mine. Then I told them there were four of us and they said to go bring my friends. I had them go up one at a time so as not to arouse the concierge's suspicions. It was a large building. There were many people in the corridors. No one paid any attention to us. When we were all together we made friends quickly. They were poor. In a large city you could live only by barter or the black market. So I gave the father four packages of tobacco and two boxes of cigars. He didn't smoke but that would be good money for barter. I gave him five thousand pesetas to get food for us. He came back loaded down and had to make a second trip. There was everything: meat, fish, melons, oranges, rice, chick-peas and white bread. The wife prepared dinner while we took showers. We shaved, shined our shoes, mended our clothes and cleaned our guns until they gleamed, especially the insides of the barrels. After that we dined on a paella the like of which we'd seldom had. At six El Grande came in. He was very happy to see me. He gave me a suit that belonged to his brother, who luckily for me was small. Then he took me to supper in a café where there were only boxers and Falangist chiefs stinking with money. El Grande drank only lemonade. I drank some vermouth. We kidded with some women, but I did nothing more than look at them. I didn't want to play around as I had decided to leave before daybreak. We came back at four in the morning. I awakened my companions. We couldn't stay in the middle of a large city. A suspicion, a denunciation, and there was sure to be a visit from the police. We had to leave before daylight.

At six we were outside. El Grande took us to the edge of the city by streets where we wouldn't meet anybody. We crossed the railroad and came to a river where there was just a ribbon of water. But all along it there were cane fields with a good path, well hidden. I gave the boxer a thousand pesetas and we parted.

By following the river we would rejoin the railroad to Zaragoza which would guide us to the route we had left. I wanted to pass through countryside I knew and cross the river Ebro where I had so often crossed it before. After that, I would be in familiar country almost all the way to the border.

By nightfall we came in sight of the city of Castellón de la Plana. By the side of the road there was a fine house all by itself. It was all lit up. Hidden behind trees, we watched it from the other side of the road. It seemed to be a kind of hotel for officers. They were almost all high-ranking Falangists. A car drove up and four Civil Guardsmen got out and went into the house after parking their car in the yard. We heard music. It had to be an officers' mess. Since they were Fascists, we were going to attack.

I made the assignments: Vicente and I would take care of the provisions, tobacco and money; Antonio and Enrique would take care of the personnel. We crossed the road and went calmly into the yard behind our two Civil Guardsmen. There were two real ones standing guard at the great door opening on a fine room. At the end of it I saw a handsome counter, and behind it a mirror and bottles. When we came to the foot of the steps, I threw a grenade into the room between the hats of Antonio and Enrique, then I shot point-blank at the two Civil Guardsmen. Vicente had thrown a grenade behind the counter and another against a door at the back. Enrique stayed at the door, Antonio surveyed the room. It was a disaster in there. I leapt over the dead and emptied the drawer of the cash register into my rucksack. Vicente opened the door at the back. He found himself nose to nose with a commandant and struck him down at once. This room was the kitchen. Rapidly he filled a sack with everything he could lay hands on. I took the tobacco and stuck bottles of rum and cognac into each of my pockets. The wounded were moaning, but they were only unarmed civilians. I finished off a Civil Guard captain. Just as I called to Vicente to leave, Enrique ran in to say a car had arrived. We hid behind the door leading inside. Two noncoms and a well-dressed civilian got out of the car. When they reached the top of the stairs we riddled them with bullets. I took their billfolds and we left at a run. A burst of tommy-gun fire came from a second-story window. Enrique was hit in the left arm. We had to get away quickly. As soon as we got to cover I hurriedly made a dressing for Enrique's arm.

We went close to the city through the gardens on a deserted side. We found a shed with a mule and some farm tools inside. We settled in. Through some trees we could see a big house so we couldn't speak loudly or make a fire. The night was bright; by leaving the door open we could count our booty. We divided the bread, cans and cold cuts. I advised eating quickly without drinking alcohol. I treated Enrique. The bullet had only grazed a muscle. I washed the wound with cognac, then made a good dressing with the gauze and he lay down by the mule. I counted the money: 74,830 pesetas in the rucksack and 14,320 in the billfolds. Thirty-one packages of cigarettes, eleven packets of tobacco, eighty-three cigars which I wrapped in a paper, plus sixteen broken cigars. I gave each man five packages of cigarettes, two cigars and a packet of tobacco. I gave the broken cigars to Enrique — he smoked like a chimney. For weapons we had captured two automatic pistols with five clips and a Mauser. I kept watch at the door while the others rested. I totaled up the balance of the attack in my head in order to write it down on my pad in the morning: three Civil Guardsmen plus a captain, seven Falangist officers, a commandant, four air force lieutenants, three captains, one civilian, a woman, and two wounded civilians. Total, twenty-one killed and two wounded. I didn't count the personnel of the hotel who were bleeding at the counter and the kitchen tables.

Before daybreak Vicente came to relieve me. I went to look at Enrique. He was not suffering, but his jacket was covered with blood. I took a pail and went to draw water from the well to wash the jacket. Day broke. I went to the end of the garden to observe the road with the binoculars. There was some traffic. I saw two ambulances pass, then a van of military police. They were looking for us. We had to keep quiet, rest and not show ourselves. About seven an old peasant appeared with a sack on his back. He was afraid when he saw us. We reassured him. We explained that we were escaped prisoners. I gave him a package of cigarettes. I made him sit down; he emptied his bag: a little piece of bread, in a pot a little rice and green beans — that was all he had to eat for the day. Then I showed him our store and invited him to eat with us. He was reassured. He explained that behind the shed there was a large garden and his job was to tend it. This morning he had to work with the mule. We let him go but Vicente watched that he didn't go to the town. You always had to be careful with civilians. At one he came back to eat with us. He went to get wine. There was a cask hidden under some straw in a small shed. Afterwards we all napped together.

In the afternoon we went to the garden to gather some vegetables for the road. I burned the billfolds. Enrique and Antonio left their rifles and cartridges, which they hid under the straw. With the two machine pistols their load was lighter. At evening we ate supper with the peasant and I gave him five hundred pesetas, two packages of cigarettes, five cigars and a sausage. He was happy. He gave me wine and a large rucksack which would be for Antonio.

When night fell we left at the same time the peasant returned to town. We were well rested and cleaned up. We could show ourselves, but we would stick to the small country roads without getting too far from the railroad line. We went slowly, avoiding as much as possible being seen by the men working on the line. We passed through orange orchards where we met women gathering fruit. We talked a bit. They said according to the newspapers there were armed bandits who attacked all along the roads. Their chief was El Mexicano. I laughed and asked for details of what the bandits did. Then they would laugh too, saying they loved to tell about him, that he surely never harmed women, and so on. . . .

The Band of El Mexicano

W E MARCHED without incident for four days and nights, resting often. Then we came in sight of a large factory. We advanced in the direction of its smokestacks. From the top of a wooded hill we saw a prison camp with huts surrounded by barbed wire and a post of soldiers at the entrance. In the woods we found a small cave; there we spent the night.

The next morning we saw a column of prisoners come out, guarded by four soldiers and a Civil Guardsman. The column returned at noon, then left again at one-thirty. There were about thirty men, still accompanied by guards. They went in the direction of the factory; the prisoners must have worked there. I followed them awhile from the woods. The column passed to one side of a bombed-out house some two miles from the camp, then took a road which must have led to the factory. At six in the evening the prisoners returned to the camp.

We slept in the cave again and in the morning went down to the bombed-out house and hid ourselves. The column arrived about seven. They were thirty, marching in files of three. Two soldiers were in front, two others on the sides; two Civil Guardsmen followed behind, sub-machine guns on their shoulders. I gave my orders. We were going to try to take ten volunteers with us. We would have to act fast as we were not far from the camp. The column came near the house. We jumped out and Enrique and I mowed down the two Civil Guardsmen. Antonio and Vicente had the soldiers raise their hands high. They were Galicians. There was an instant of panic among the prisoners. I asked if there were ten volunteers to escape. I would lead them to France. I needed young ones, for it would be hard. Five stepped out at once, then another group of six. I gave them the weapons of the four soldiers and the two Civil Guardsmen, had the two bodies put inside the house and ordered the remaining prisoners to go into the house and stay there until it was time to go back to the camp. When they got back they could tell what had happened. I gave them five packets of tobacco and ten cigars. I told the four soldiers we meant them no harm but they would have to come with us for a while. Then we went back to the cave.

From up there I watched the camp through the binoculars. The prisoners from the column must not have obeyed my orders. It was like an anthill down there with men running around in all directions. Patrols circled the camp, rifles in hand. We had to move fast. I went over to the four soldiers. They were afraid I was going to kill them. I told them I didn't kill soldiers. I made them undress, except for one who declared he wanted to join us. Three of the liberated prisoners exchanged their clothes with those of the soldiers. While they dressed, Antonio took down their names, their provinces, whether they could read and write. There were four Andalusians, four Asturians, two Valencians, one Catalan and one Galician. The oldest was thirty. They had all been Republican soldiers, except for two who were political prisoners. The three soldiers, now dressed as prisoners, were well treated: I left them their watches, their money, their cigarettes — but these they shared themselves with the liberated prisoners.

We prepared to leave. They were all astonished when they saw our armament. I distributed weapons, saying those who were afraid of adventure could still return to the camp. We were going to go on fighting for the Republic while on the way to France. The enemy was everywhere but we were passing through country which had been Republican, where the war had not been over long and where the Francoists were still not organized. We had a chance to get through if we always kept moving, and I explained that I knew the tactics because I had been the leader of a group which operated behind enemy lines. Whatever happened, we would fight to the death. I also distributed tobacco and provisions so that each had his share to carry. Then we left.

At the end of some three miles, I freed the three soldiers, asking them for the sake of their deserting buddy not to go back to camp until evening. They could say they got lost. We left them, and as soon as they were out of sight we changed direction.

Two of the prisoners knew the region and we followed their directions. All these men were young, but they had been poorly fed and their shoes were worn out. We had to go slowly and rest often. As they had no experience marching as guerrillas I had them go in groups of five spaced only ten yards apart so they wouldn't get lost, and also because several were scared: they looked around all the time and thought they saw the enemy everywhere. When I went ahead as scout, I took one with me to teach him the job and also to watch how he behaved. I explained that when you were numerous, you must not let yourself be surprised, and I taught him the signals for warning from a distance without calling. Behind, Vicente did the same: no loud talking, laughing, singing or arguing. If you wanted to stay alive you always had to be on the lookout.

We went along a path that followed the wheat fields and orchards. We picked fruit. It had been a long time since the prisoners had seen any. I explained that you had to eat calmly and take only enough to eat on the way, for you must never load yourself too much. That way you wouldn't get tired and you could keep lively in your movements. There was plenty of water flowing in all the ditches. The corn was ripe. We took some and stopped to roast it between two rocks. They all ate their fill. They began to find that freedom tasted good. Toward evening we came in view of a farm. It had an isolated barn. I went to reconnoiter: it was full of straw, a good place to sleep. But we would have to wait for nightfall; the farm wasn't far away. We settled down and I gave my instructions: the least tired would stand guard. We would have to keep circling around the place where we camped. At night a surprise is always deadly. The man on guard must shake any men snoring loud; at night the noise could be heard far. Also he must prevent smokers from lighting a cigarette: the light of a match could be seen over a mile.

The night passed very quietly. In my corner I didn't sleep much. Now we were sixteen, a good number. But we had to form the group into a real troop, study the capabilities of each man, learn maneuvers, the use of weapons — the whole trade. I wouldn't be happy for some days, because it is better to have five trained men than fifteen who have no experience of combat.

I reviewed the state of the band of El Mexicano:

FRANCISCO, EL MEXICANO, French volunteer, 1 automatic, 1 submachine gun, 2 daggers

VICENTE, 1st lieutenant, Republican, 1 automatic, 1 submachine gun, 2 daggers

ENRIQUE, 2nd lieutenant, Republican, 1 automatic, 1 submachine gun, 1 switchblade knife

ANTONIO, 3rd lieutenant, Republican, 1 automatic, 1 submachine gun, 1 switchblade knife

MIER, freed prisoner, Asturian, Republican, 1 automatic, dress: soldier

MENDOZA, freed prisoner, Asturian, Republican, 1 automatic, 2 cartridges, dress: soldier

PLANERO, freed prisoner, Basque, Republican, 1 automatic, 3 cartridges, dress: soldier

LUIS, freed prisoner, Basque, Republican, 1 automatic, 2 cartridges, dress: prisoner

MANUEL, freed prisoner, Sevilla, Republican, 1 automatic, 2 cartridges, dress: prisoner

JOSÉ, freed prisoner, Córdoba, Republican, 1 automatic, 3 cartridges, dress: prisoner

SANCHEZ, freed prisoner, Sevilla, Republican, 1 automatic, 2 cartridges, dress: prisoner

LUIS, freed prisoner, Málaga, Republican, 1 rifle, 1 bayonet, dress: prisoner

PEDRO, freed prisoner, Valencia, Republican, 1 rifle, 1 bayonet, dress: prisoner

QUADIOLA, freed prisoner, Sueca, Republican, 1 rifle, dress: prisoner

ANTONIO, freed prisoner, Catalonian mulatto from Vich, 1 rifle, dress: prisoner

MECHOL, Francoist soldier, Lugo, unarmed

At sunup, while the men prepared to leave I observed the surroundings with my binoculars. The view was good. I saw four Civil Guardsmen advancing on horseback along the path towards the farm. It was time for a good ambush. I took Vicente, Enrique, Antonio and also Mechol, the Francoist soldier, after explaining his part to him. The others stayed hidden in the barn, ready to help us. We were going to hide in the bushes on either side of the path. Mechol, the Galician, unarmed, was on the path pretending to retie his shoelaces. The guardsmen approached, looking to the right and left. In turning a corner they came upon Mechol who attracted their attention. At once we each fired on our designated victim. Then we undressed them: we took their uniforms, their hats and their shoes, which my new men needed especially. We took their weapons: two rifles, four automatics with eleven clips, two machine guns with four clips, three watches, and a pair of binoculars the corporal carried.

The shots had aroused the people at the farm. They barricaded themselves. But an old woman came towards us; I told her they had nothing to fear, she must go and bring us all the bread they had and something to drink. We did not want their money. On the contrary we would pay, and I gave her a thousand pesetas. She returned to the farm and came back with two young men. One carried a sack of round loaves of bread, the other a sack filled with a little of everything.

While Mechol and Enrique carried the sacks to the barn, Antonio and I tied two of the horses to a tree; a third was wounded and I killed it with a bullet in the head so it wouldn't suffer. Unfortunately the fourth had run away and that was dangerous: if he went back where he had come from he would give the alert.

All my band came out of the barn, ready to depart. I distributed the weapons: a submachine gun to Mier, an automatic to Quadiola, a submachine gun to Mechol, the Francoist. He was happy that I had confidence in him; he had thought he would never be armed because I would consider him a traitor. I gave an automatic to Antonio the black. We took the ammunition for the rifles but broke the rifles themselves against a tree. I distributed the shoes: the men they fit got them. Then we left; it was high time.

We walked down the road about two miles, then passed through the fields back to the farm. Without showing ourselves we slipped into the barn and waited. I explained to the new ones that after a raid you must never run through the countryside. You pretend to escape and then come back to lie low at the place of the raid and wait until those who are chasing you are far away. About one o'clock two vans loaded with Civil Guardsmen arrived, at least twenty of them. From the gestures of the peasants they interrogated we understood that they told them we had left by the hill road. The guardsmen looked all around, then they took away the bodies; two untied the horses and mounted them, others loaded the dead horse on a third van which had arrived. Then they left on the road in the direction indicated by the peasants. Only two Civil Guardsmen remained. They went up to the farm and went in. They surely intended to find out everything in detail. After a while they came out with the old woman who led them to the place where they gave us the sacks. Then one of the guardsmen drew his automatic and went back to the farm. He came back pushing the two young men who had carried the sacks. I understood; they were going to execute them on the same spot. Quickly Vicente and I hurried behind the barn. We arrived just as one of the guardsmen shot the old woman, who fell on her knees. The instant he turned to the two men I fired at him and Vicente fired too. By the time the other fired his tommy gun my knife was in him. Unfortunately the two peasants didn't have the presence of mind to throw themselves to the ground. In falling the Civil Guardsman had fired a burst and the peasants were mowed down. The people from the house ran up and I explained what had happened. They took away their dead without saying a word. I undressed the two Civil Guardsmen, took their automatics and ammunition, their shoes, pants and 428 pesetas that I found in their pockets. I gave one automatic to Luis, the other to Pedro. Now everyone was well armed and well shod. We left again.

The six men dressed as Civil Guardsmen marched in front in double file, as was the custom of real Civil Guardsmen on patrol. I was at the head of our single file, the soldiers marching half in front, half behind the prisoners, as though they were guarding them. Vicente followed, dressed as a peasant, twenty yards behind.

We marched all day along the flanks of the hills. Towards evening we came to a large plain. The terrain was open: nothing but dry grass and gravel. With the binoculars I spotted a forest on the other side, about six miles away. A road ran along the edge of the forest and beyond it there was a mountain we would have to get to. It was too late to cross the plain. The moon had risen. In its light the enemy could have seen us but I could not have seen them if they had been on the road passing in the shadow of the trees. Better combat by day than an ambush at night.

We settled for the night in the shelter of a rock. We couldn't make a fire. A sentinel watched the path we had come along. We all sat in a circle and I explained the instructions in case of combat; I again explained the meaning of the various yells and the signals I would make with the arms and fingers. I made each one repeat them. I explained what you must do if you were lost; how you must never attack alone, but always with the help of several comrades to cover you; how you must not panic if you were surrounded; it was very easy to escape if you kept a cool head. Above all never run away: you became the rabbit for the hunter. You must always be the hunter, always go forward attacking, and always rest before the dangerous moments; a tired man is a bad fighter. Afterwards we ate all we had with us, sharing it piece by piece; we emptied a canteen of wine and slept.

We set out well rested at daybreak. We crossed in the same formation. I was in the lead, stopping often to observe. We were a little over a mile from the forest when I saw a patrol of seven Civil Guardsmen on horseback come out of the forest and advance towards us. I looked all around the plain: another patrol on horseback was advancing behind us. They wanted to catch us between two lines of fire. I ordered a pause for catching our breath. I went through all the signals again to make sure everybody understood them well. Our morale was good. Then we started guerrilla style toward the forest. The seven Civil Guardsmen advanced on us and soon opened fire with carbines. We went forward by spurts, rapidly, without firing. When they were almost on us each fired according to his instructions, some at the horses, others at the men. The guardsmen were thrown to the ground. All of a sudden the black Catalan was overcome with fear and took off for the forest. He was soon shot and killed by one of the guardsmen. The others followed me all right, moving in quick dashes, and we made the forest just as the other patrol in full gallop began firing at us from behind. But now we were well sheltered. Mechol, the Francoist soldier, was at my side; he fired his tommy gun in short bursts but always straight. He was a good fighter. The battle lasted ten minutes. Some of the guardsmen came into the woods. All at once one came right at me, tommy gun in hand. Vicente, who by now knew the drill and was covering me, sprang from behind and felled him with a bullet in the neck. All the Civil Guardsmen had been killed except two who rode away at a gallop. Unfortunately, in the heat of the battle we had fired on one of our Civil Guardsmen at a moment when he was fighting with a real one. I lost the black and two others; I had a third gravely wounded. He was dying and I finished him with a bullet in the head so he wouldn't suffer. Each did his job: collecting everything while some kept watch. Then we regrouped and advanced to the cover of the trees but following the edge of the forest so as to watch the plain. A little farther on we rested in a clearing. Manuel had had his left hand shot through by a bullet; I made him a dressing. Meanwhile the others brought together what we had found in the saddlebags. No provisions, but sub-machine guns and lots of ammunition. With that our men were saved. Four men had died for the Republic: Luis of Málaga, Planero the Basque, Quadiola of Sueca and the Catalan from Vich, a fine comrade but a poor soldier. I gave notice that after this when engaged in combat our Civil Guardsmen would throw their hats aside and turn their sleeves back, and I had them rip the seams.

We advanced keeping under cover and watching the plain, so that we could see the enemy and also find a farm to revictual as we had nothing left. As night fell we at last came in sight of a large farm. We approached and while our comrades surrounded it Vicente and I looked in the windows. The farmers were at supper. They must have been poor as the table was lit by little earthenware oil lamps. We knocked on the door. An old man answered. When he saw our weapons he understood, but he was not afraid. He let us in. When I saw there was plenty to eat and drink I went back out and gave the rally call. Everyone came in except those who stood guard. In one corner the young women stood silently, just looking at us. Happily the older ones busied themselves preparing us a good meal: a good cabbage soup with bacon and fried eggs. Meanwhile the old man filled two large packs with bread and meat and gave me two gourds of wine. I asked to buy some peasant clothes; he brought me three old but still good pairs of pants

215

and two jackets. When we had eaten, they fed the two sentinels. I gave the old man a thousand pesetas and a package of tobacco. These people were brave but dumfounded: they didn't say three words to us the whole time we were there. We took the mountain path and when we came to the top we slept under the guard of two sentinels.

In the morning we awoke in a deep forest. From the other side of the mountain you couldn't see a road or a house, nothing but trees. We had food and a little tobacco. We marched quietly, not talking. Everything was fine except for Manuel, who was in pain from his hand, but the wound was clean and he marched without a pack. We went all day without meeting anyone. From time to time we startled hares and even wild boars by the path. We went on like that for three days. By then we were eating sweet acorns, wild apples and even some tender grass. We couldn't risk firing at a hare. Then we came to the end of the forest. Now there were well-cultivated hillsides with numerous farmhouses and we saw villages in the valley. According to Sánchez, our scout, we were approaching Zaragoza. We were entering a former Republican zone, but even so we would have to be careful of the peasants. Near the towns there were many Civil Guardsmen and the peasants spied to stay in good with the authorities. But we were weak from lack of food. I decided to set up an ambush on the road rather than to risk asking at a farm.

We descended to a small road. We took positions on both sides of it, well hidden by the ditches and trees. Many peasants passed with loaded mules; we let them go on. Finally a truck with the insignia of the military administration appeared. I gave the cry of attack. The driver was killed at once and the truck went into the ditch. What luck! It was filled with groceries. We filled our five packs with everything at hand, took two sacks of round loaves of bread, some bottles of wine and cognac. I told Vicente to take a bag full of canvas shoes like the ones legionnaires wear; the soles were woven rope, very good for marching in the mountains. A sergeant sitting beside the driver had been killed too. On his knees I found a small metal box full of money. We could use it. Vicente stopped a small car. Two peasants were carrying chickens and baskets of onions. I took five chickens and a sack of onions, gave them a thousand pesetas and we were saved.

We rejoined our comrades and the whole troop climbed back up to the woods where we found an abandoned hut with a fireplace. We set four sentinels, made a good fire and roasted the chickens. We drank wine and a little cognac. I gave each man three cigarettes. I counted the money in the metal box: 33,400 pesetas. I gave the men two pairs of canvas shoes apiece and threw away the rest. Then I went with Sánchez to relieve the sentinels.

That evening we left well rested and everyone was cheerful. But the mountains of Zaragoza are not like the seaside of Valencia; the night is cold. Except for Vicente, who was wearing corduroy, we all had canvas on our backs and no blankets. We could not light a fire. So we preferred to keep marching with short pauses to drink a little cognac. Fortunately in the morning we came on a group of woodcutters. They had a good fire. We cooked red sausages and made good hot sandwiches. We gave some to the five woodcutters and soon we were good friends. They said there were still four villages before the road to Zaragoza. The first was full of legionnaires; each of the others was guarded by four Civil Guardsmen and besides there were patrols on the roads leading to the mountains. The farms were rich in pork and black bread. But the villagers were miserly and suspicious. They would have to be taken by force. We stayed with the woodcutters all day; in the evening they invited us to sleep in their hut. We were packed, but we were warm; there were sacks of straw and blankets. We roasted a hare they had caught in a trap and given us. When it was time to leave they gave us their blankets saying they could go get others in the village. I gave each one two thousand pesetas. They had never seen so much money at one time.

We put the blankets in two sacks. The men who carried them marched in the rear. We came to a spring the woodcutters had told us about: it flowed forming a stream* we were to follow. We came in view of a village; it was swarming with soldiers. Little by little the stream became a pretty little river bordered by gardens. We gathered fruit, tomatoes, peppers and lettuce, and a few miles further on found an isolated barn full of straw and hay. We moved in and ate the fresh vegetables without oil or salt. We hadn't had vegetables for several days. We spent a good night. The next day we came close to the second village, Villanueva. We met two women with a peasant on the path. At first they were

---

*An estuary of the river Huerva which empties into the Ebro at Zaragoza. V. G.

afraid. We spoke politely to them. They said they were going to work at a large farm where we might get some provisions as the farmer was a brave, good man. We followed them. They went into the farm. After a few minutes two peasants arrived with sacks. The women had spoken the truth: there were eight large loaves of bread, a ham, three cheeses and some sausages. I gave the peasants three thousand pesetas. Mier and Vicente went back with them to ask if they could sell us some oil and vinegar, some wine and the three blankets we still needed. They came back with everything, and a three-liter gourd of vermouth to boot. Then I went to the farm to thank the owner, and gave him three thousand pesetas. He told me to be very careful of the patrols of legionnaires who were on maneuvers in the mountains, pillaging and causing a reign of terror.

We ate on the spot and then went up the mountain again, following the river at a distance. I advanced slowly with much prudence. At the slightest noise we hid. We let some civilians pass, as well as legionnaires going along talking in groups of two or three. When we came to the top of the mountain I looked all around with the binoculars. There were camps of soldiers with tents everywhere. Military convoys and even some tanks passed along the highway. We crossed the river by a small wooden bridge, got across the highway and climbed up the other mountain. Near the top we found some old trenches.* We had only to bend over to gather

---

*Francisco was near Villanueva, which had marked the farthest point of the Republican army's advance in their August 1937 campaign to take Zaragoza. V. G.

German grenades with wooden handles or Lafite bombs
with strings. We even found a machine gun. We took it
apart; it was a bit rusty in places and as we had vinegar
we took it apart piece by piece, cleaned it well, greased
it with butter and put it back together. There were bullets in profusion. We fitted it with five drums. There
were so many troops in the region that we didn't hesitate
to try it on a paper target; it fired a little to the left and
had a tendency to rise. I gave the gun to Luis, who was
stocky. But by bad luck it began to rain. We took refuge
in an army shelter. It rained without stop all night and
the next day. The trenches were filled with water, but
we were dry. We spent another night. The next day we
left. The mud stuck to our shoes.

On descending the other side of the mountain we
found a road. We followed it in the direction of the village. We crossed a fine avenue of chestnut trees and
rested a bit in their shade. The avenue led to an old
abandoned convent. I sent Sánchez, José and Mechol to
inspect the place. They came running back. It was full
of soldiers inside and there were two trucks. We made
a detour to get back to the mountain. We were climbing
a path: the two trucks came out of the convent; one
stopped at the foot of our path to let out legionnaires;
the other stopped farther toward the right. I grasped
their tactic: they wanted to encircle us. I gave the order
to descend to the rear of the convent. Since the trucks
had left there wouldn't be many men there, just officers
and some guards. They were legionnaires, but we were
Republican volunteers; we were equally armed and we
were going to counterattack.

Slipping from bush to bush we came up behind the

convent, which now appeared rather to be an old castle. At the foot of the wall enclosing it we unloaded our packs and canteens. Pedro and José, who carried the blankets, stayed to guard the supplies and cover our rear. While the legionnaires were hunting us in the mountains we were going to attack the castle. I gave my instructions: ten of us would attack. Four would come with me on the left side, four on the right under the lead of Vicente. There were two sentinels at the large gate opening on the courtyard. On turning the corner of the castle, Vicente would hit them with a grenade. At the same moment I would turn my corner of the castle and we would leap into the interior. I would throw grenades, then we would mount to the second story while Vicente finished off those below. We had to make sure we cleaned out the whole façade so that we wouldn't be fired on from the windows of the upper floor.

We went through the wall of the enclosure at a point where it had given way a bit; then we separated, each to his own side. On the left was a flower garden and there were no windows on this side of the building. We advanced behind shrubs and banks of flowers. The two sentinels were at the gate. At this moment a lieutenant came out of the castle and walked toward the sentinels. I gave my Mexican "Hai." The grenades exploded. We leaped into the entrance of the castle. There was a large stone stairway. On the left a door was open on an office full of officers. We threw two grenades in and dashed up the stairs. At a window on the landing a legionnaire was firing a machine gun down at Manuel, the Andalusian — who, disobeying orders, had gone to the wounded sentinels at the gate to finish them off. We took the legionnaire from behind and he crumpled. We went into a room to the left. It was a mess hall. Four unarmed legionnaires raised their hands. We killed them. On the right there was no one. We came back down. In the office I found the bodies of three commandants, two captains and two lieutenants. On the other side, in the kitchen, Vicente was already putting everything into a sack. But two of our men were on the ground, dead: Antonio, my third lieutenant, and Mendoza, the Asturian, who had been a brave fighter. They had been surprised by five legionnaires in the kitchen while Vicente was finishing off the officers. One of my men had a tommy gun and had time to fire a burst before falling. Vicente had killed the other legionnaires and also two Alsatian wolfhounds tied to a table. I said to gather everything fast. In the entry where the arms were we stuffed our pockets with very good pineapple grenades; we took the machine gun with three drums, some caps and capes, and left the way we came, after setting fire everywhere.

I quickly had Vicente and four other men dress in the caps and capes of the legionnaires. One man even had an officer's helmet. While we loaded our packs, they ran to the truck which was still at the foot of the path. The two men guarding it let them approach unsuspecting. They were killed. Luis, who was a good driver, took the wheel and brought the truck back to the castle. We got in, the truck turned into the avenue and once on the highway we sped toward Zaragoza. The castle was full of smoke and we could see the legionnaires running down the mountain.

The back of the truck contained capes, jackets and a case of new boots. We put boots on our feet and took as many as we could carry. We had captured a machine gun with three drums, twenty-two grenades, five capes, three pairs of leather boots and 4,800 pesetas. Mechol had carried a case of tobacco from the castle. We quickly filled our packs. There were also ten loaves of bread, at least twenty pounds of sausages, sardines and canned beef. The attack had been good, but we had lost three good comrades.

The truck made good speed. We passed peasants with their mules, a motorbike and several trucks. Pedro, who had done his military service at Zaragoza, knew the road. A little before entering the city he turned the truck down a small road. We drove through the countryside until we came to a small wood. There we hid the truck behind the trees. We got out and once we had our packs well arranged we started up the low mountain in order to go around the city and turn toward the river Ebro, which I wanted to cross at a place I knew. According to my information, to get there we had to follow the large electric power line which ran from Zaragoza to Barcelona. It passed over deserted mountains in which you would be lost if you got far away from the line. We were marching in two groups of four spaced ten yards apart. Vicente went ahead as scout. Night fell. We stopped at an isolated hut. As the truck was well hidden, it wouldn't be found before morning. We could rest well; here there was no risk.

We left again at dawn. From the top of the mountain the city was visible. I looked at the railroad station with the binoculars; it was swarming with activity. Then we came down toward the highway to Barcelona to look for the plant that the power line started from. When we came in sight of the power line, we passed many people. Because of our legionnaires' caps, our weapons and our beards, everyone was afraid of us. When we passed by houses the people ran and locked themselves in. I sent Pedro and Vicente to a tavern. They ordered ham, sausage and cheese sandwiches and wine. Meanwhile I looked all around. When Vicente called, we went in. We ate and drank. Then I went over to the bartender; I ordered a bottle of oil, five packets of tobacco and ten of cigarettes. Without asking for the bill I gave him 2,500 pesetas. He was delighted.

We had found the line, we were all fed, and we turned into the mountains. We climbed by a small path. All at once Vicente signaled that four Civil Guardsmen were advancing towards us on horseback. We set up an ambush. We threw a grenade at the first horse and killed the riders of the others with a volley. We took two submachine guns and hurried on, as we were still in view of the highway.

The mountain was bare; no trees, only rocks and caves where poor people lived. When we got to the top we rested three hours. We were too heavily loaded. I decided that we would keep only our weapons, a blanket apiece, and light provisions. I would carry the reserve of tobacco, the money, a bottle of oil and one of cognac. The men wanted to abandon the two heavy machine guns. I said we would do that farther on; for the moment we were in a region too full of soldiers and Civil Guardsmen. We could get ourselves killed if we were surprised by a well-armed enemy.

According to Pedro we would have to climb over another rocky mountain and then we would be marching under pines and oaks. We set off. Fortunately we were now a bit lighter. The climb was hard. We had to scale large rocks, and a cold wind was blowing. We were lucky to be well clothed and shod. We were almost to the summit when Vicente, going ahead as scout, signaled an enemy troop. We hid behind some rocks with a machine gun on either side of the trail, ready to fire. It was a column of twenty legionnaires marching single file with a captain in the lead. From their uniforms they were Germans. When they were ten yards away I cried "Hai" and the two machine guns mowed them all down. Then we threw ourselves body to body to finish them off. At that moment six or seven more legionnaires, who had been following behind, ran up firing. They were real fighters. They hurled themselves at us and fought like lions. We won, but four of ours lay dead. I went from one to the other. Luis the Basque had taken a bullet in the forehead, Sánchez, my Andalusian scout, had his head blown off by a grenade, José the Cordovan had got a burst in the belly. Pedro had been killed from behind by several bayonet stabs. Now we were only five. I redivided the arms: Vicente, Antonio and Mechol the Galician each took four grenades, their submachine guns, an automatic, three boxes of bullets and three clips. Mier the Basque, the heftiest of us, carried the machine gun, too, but no provisions. When we got to the summit I saw the wooded mountain Pedro had spoken of, and through the binoculars I could see the power line stretching in the distance across the mountains.

225

Across the Ebro

OUR PACKS were full of provisions, we had plenty of water, a bottle of cognac, oil and vinegar and my pharmacy. We marched through the mountains without losing sight of the power line. We rested often. In spite of our losses our morale was good. In a valley below I spied a farm through the binoculars. Horses, cows and a herd of sheep grazed around it. Going down toward the farm we met a small boy guarding a herd of goats. He knew nothing of the war and came toward us without fear. I asked if he could sell us some milk. He said he would find as much as we wanted at the farm. I got him to talk about the owner. The boy said he was head of the district and very mean: he always had a rifle on his arm and if anyone came who didn't belong to the farm, he had them arrested, and the Civil Guardsmen who came through every two days about noon to get food led them away and they were never seen again. I gave the boy a hundred pesetas and we went down to the farm.

I sent Vicente ahead, his tommy gun well hidden under his jacket. When he came to the gate he called loudly. A man of about fifty came out with a hunting rifle in his hand. He was well dressed in new corduroys. He asked Vicente what he wanted. Vicente answered he was looking for work. The man asked for his papers and his certificate from the Civil Guard. Vicente said he had them in his jacket. Then the man lowered his gun. He called and two men came out, also armed with rifles. He told them to take Vicente to the stable, examine his papers, and if they were in order to put him to work in the lower field. Hidden behind a hedge, I heard everything. Vicente was in danger. I made a sign; we leapt over the hedge and ran forward yelling. Vicente threw himself to the ground and fired his automatic. I killed the owner with a burst. Antonio and Mier had done the same to the two men. Then seven unarmed men ran out of the farm with their hands in the air crying we were their saviors. We went in the farmhouse while Mechol undressed the Falangist leader to take his clothes. The farm women brought a ham, sausages, a cheese and round loaves of bread. The little shepherd, who had come running at the sound of the shots, brought us a pitcher full of milk. We all drank. Mechol made a bundle of the fine clothes of the owner and gave me 1,300 pesetas that he had found in the pockets. I gave them to the farmhands and added four thousand pesetas because the woman and child had been so kind.

We set off behind the farm. We had gone a half a mile when we saw two Civil Guardsmen on horseback. We let them approach and fired a volley. The first fell; the second, wounded, turned his horse and fled towards the farm. He would find a surprise.

We climbed back up the mountain. The nights were too cold to sleep outside. Each evening we sought the shelter of a cave, a hut or a demolished house. There were many of these, for we were entering Catalonia. The country was wild, with real forests. Soon we came on old trenches, in sight of the sierras where I had fought and been taken prisoner. We collected grenades. There were still corpses that were now almost skeletons. The peasants were working in their fields. They seemed to be miserable and afraid. They said there were Civil Guardsmen everywhere. When we had eaten all our provisions we went down to the river; I threw a grenade in one deep pool and we got some fine fish. We grilled them and had a feast. In the gardens we still found dried figs and olives on the ground and occasionally some potatoes. We marched like that for several days, peacefully enough but with low morale. I explained that once we were past the Ebro the country would be richer and less devastated and the people would be more hospitable. Then we came to a large village. I sent on Vicente with Mechol, well dressed in the new corduroy. They soon came back to get us. The baker would put us up. We spent the night close to the oven and had a warm sleep. We could wash, shave and cut our hair. At supper we ate a pot of broad-bean meal mixed with salt pork and all the bread we wanted. We left at dawn all braced up by the hospitality of the baker. I gave him a thousand pesetas. He filled our canteens with wine and our packs were stuffed with as much bread as they could hold.

We went on by a path across the fields. We were glad to be clean, well rested, and well fed. But there was no denying we were demoralized from trudging along many days without attacking. I saw that we would have to find an opportunity.

We advanced, observing often with the binoculars. Antonio had taken Sánchez's and did the same as I. We watched a little farm for two hours. We saw two peasants leave; then a woman came out to sit in the sun by the door. Two children played with a white goat. I sent on Mechol and Vicente. Vicente spoke Catalan. They talked to the woman and made a sign for us to come too. They were poor peasants who made their bread with corn meal. We stayed with them two days and three nights to rest up well and be in good condition for the crossing of the Ebro, which might be difficult. We lent a hand with the work and cut some wood. The woman gave us a large loaf of cornbread. I paid her a thousand pesetas. We left in good shape.

We were approaching Gandesa. I was back in familiar country. The mountains were barer and full of ravines and gorges. On the heights there were trenches still full of grenades and rusty weapons. From time to time there were wooden crosses without names: some ours and some the Nationalists'. We often came on burnt-out remains of trucks and tanks. We found some dried figs and almonds in the gorges. In one garden we even found some tomatoes, though they were a bit rotten. Fortunately we still had bread; it was hard as a rock, but it tasted good.

We went around a village and soon afterwards I recognized the mill where I had been locked up for two days without food or water. I sent on Vicente and Mechol. A peasant told them that the owner of the mill was a Falangist leader, very rich and very mean. He owned more than half of Gandesa. He lived at the first farm on the right. He was always guarded by two Civil Guardsmen. We continued down the road and after two miles we saw the farm. It was more like a château, with a park and grapevines. We spoke to a peasant. He said that the leader lived in the château and that we would have to be careful — there were two fierce wolfhounds. No one could get in without a pass from the Civil Guard.

Here was our chance to attack. We walked around the park and hid waiting for night. When it was dark we advanced tree by tree. At two hundred yards from the manor house we heard the dogs, but they were locked in a kennel. They must have scented us: they bayed and bayed. A Civil Guardsman came out of the château and went to call to the dogs. He looked all around and then sat down on a bench near the door. But as it was cold he didn't stay long.

I planned the attack. On the side of the house there was a window. Mier and Mechol would take their post there, ready to attack with grenades. Vicente and Antonio would go in by the door when the Civil Guardsmen came out. When they started firing inside, Mier and Mechol would throw their grenades through the window and go in in their turn. I would stay outside to cover them. Everything being well prepared, we threw rocks against the door of the kennel. The dogs howled. Two Civil Guardsmen came out swearing, leaving the door open. When the guardsmen got to the kennel, I killed them with a burst. Vicente and Antonio ran to the door. An instant later I heard the grenades explode. Mier and Mechol had gone in through the window. I heard shots. I didn't move from behind my tree. I watched the entrance, the windows and also my rear. Suddenly a Civil Guardsman appeared in a lower window, trying to escape. I let him jump and he ran towards me to get into the shelter of the trees. When he was ten yards away I killed him.

Now the manor house was quiet. There were a few cries, then nothing. My friends were a long time coming back. What were they doing? But I couldn't leave my post, for it was not the moment to let myself be surprised. Finally Mier and Antonio came out, each carrying a sack. Mier, tommy gun in hand, was pushing the Falangist leader in front of him. Vicente and Mechol were watching the door. I watched the windows ready to fire at a shadow. When Mier and Antonio were under cover of the trees, the others ran up. We left at once across the park. Beyond there was a small forest. When we reached it I killed the Falangist chief. We advanced into the forest. Antonio's sack was bulging all over. Curious, I asked him what was inside. He stopped, plunged his hand inside and handed me rolls. They were *bono*, rolls made with milk. It was the first time in my life I had eaten them. We were already far away when the glow of a large fire appeared behind us. Vicente before leaving had set fire to the kitchen with a can of gasoline. I asked him what had happened to the other inhabitants. He told me he had left two old women, four workmen and two children at the open door with orders not to come out for several minutes, otherwise we would fire on them. I said he did very well. You had to respect women, children and the aged, even if they were relatives of our enemies.

The night was bright. We advanced slowly because we were loaded down and a bit tired. We found a hut in an olive grove. We settled in, then we emptied the sacks and took inventory. There were twenty-two *bono* and some white bread and a smoked ham. I decided we would eat the ham right away as it was heavy to carry. There were also two boxes of big cigars, five packets of tobacco and two cartons of cigarettes. Mechol gave me the money: I counted 117,000 pesetas in hundred notes, all new. In the billfold of the Fascist I found 4,220 pesetas. His identity card said he was judge at the military tribunal of Zaragoza, commandant of the region and Falangist chief of Gandesa. We had eliminated a big bandit. When we had divided everything and I had made my accounts, we slept quite contentedly.

The next morning we set off. Not through the mountains; when reinforcements came it would be there that they would look for us. We had to fool them by staying on the plain. We passed through orchards keeping hidden in ditches. Above all we had to avoid showing ourselves to civilians, even to shepherds, who often had to report to the Civil Guardsmen each evening. Fortunately there were many abandoned houses along the road and the fields were full of the wooden sheds and earthen huts where peasants left their implements. There was always straw and hay; sometimes we found a fireplace. Then we would spend a good night: we would light a fire after putting a cape over the door. If there was a window we covered it too. The fire gave us light. One of us was always outside walking around our hiding place to avoid ambush.

One morning, hidden in some bushes at the edge of the road, we saw some twenty trucks full of Civil Guardsmen pass by. We didn't move. A moment later we saw a patrol of six Civil Guardsmen on horseback coming. They rode in threes on either side of the road surveying the countryside. We didn't move. We were well hidden in our thicket. They passed close by us without suspecting we were there. Later eleven trucks full of *Requetés,* the Red Berets. They sped rapidly toward the mountains. We saw them stop after a mile. Through the binoculars I saw them get out, then ascend by all the paths on our left. We still didn't move. Then we saw the patrol of Civil Guardsmen on horseback coming back toward us. They led two civilians in peasant dress. I couldn't free them; there were too many troops all around. Then the weather changed. It began to rain. Luckily we each had a piece of tarpaulin with a hole cut out for the head. Nothing got muddy but the bottoms of our pantlegs. We left, still keeping to the fields and avoiding the mountains. We crept behind low walls which kept us out of sight from the road. Then we saw a lot of trucks a quarter of a mile ahead of us. We flattened ourselves behind some fig trees. The rain poured twice as hard. Then a curious thing happened: we saw all the Civil Guardsmen and soldiers come tumbling down the mountain, all muddy. They jumped into the trucks which turned back in all haste to Gandesa.

The trucks had been parked beside an old house. It was surely their headquarters. When all was quiet we advanced. We went into the house. We found an old man and two young civilians dead of bayonet wounds. They were still warm. We carried their bodies to a room on one side. There they had killed a poor old woman. The fire was still burning in the fireplace. We went down to look in the cellar; there were two small casks of wine, some figs on a board, a cupboard full of food and two large loaves of bread.

While one of us stood watch at the door, we began eating and warming ourselves by the fire. Suddenly we heard a noise in the room: it came from a barrel in the corner. We looked in; the barrel was filled with sawdust. We groped in it. Then a boy about twelve came out. He was frightened and crying. We pulled him out of the barrel, consoled him and gave him food. We gave him some water. I spoke softly to him, caressed him and asked how all this had happened.

He told me he had been drinking his bowl of milk as he did every morning. "The trucks came. They demanded our papers. My father said he hadn't been able to go to Gandesa to change his pass yet. Then grandfather said, 'Why do we need them, these papers? We work for ourselves and we never leave the house.' Then they left leading my father and grandfather to take them to Gandesa. At that moment the trucks of Red Berets arrived. One of the Civil Guardsmen said, pointing to father and grandfather, 'These men are Reds; we found two rifles in the cellar.' Then they started stabbing them. They took my mother to the woods behind the house."

I asked, "And these two peasants whose bodies we found in the kitchen?"

He replied, "They were neighbors who came to help us. They hit them, then killed them with their big knives."

I sent Vicente and Mier to look behind the house. They found the mother in the woods dead, full of bayonet wounds. When I had seen and heard all that, I understood why the people were full of fear. Terror reigned here.

I thought, what shall we do with this child? To take him with us is too dangerous. To leave him would also be dangerous for him. What to do? It was time for us to go. When the child saw we were getting ready to go, he got a rucksack, filled it with goat cheeses, and added a hunk of bread. He was going to come with us.

His name was Fernando. He was always at my side. He marched well and was very tough. And he knew the mountains well; he had watched the goats there.

We came to a large farm. He told me it was abandoned. During the war it had been an officers' mess. We approached: no one. But the fields around it were cultivated. We rested a bit. We set out again and soon were in view of Corbera. The boy knew the area well. I did too; it was the village where I had been captured during the battle of the Ebro.

I observed the terrain through the binoculars. In the valley it was too flat and we had to avoid passing too close to the town. The hills were good, well wooded. But there were too many soldiers and Civil Guardsmen out there looking for us. We would go between the highway and the hills, following the smaller roads.

We went around the town. Then we advanced following the bed of a little river which ran along the road. The boy told us it was called the Rin. He was no trouble and kept up with us easily. Like us he ate anything we could find. He was quick to hide as soon as he saw anyone, and once he was in the bushes he didn't stumble. I taught him to use an automatic and a dagger; he showed me how to make a slingshot. Whenever we found a little bottle I filled it with gravel and had him throw it at a tree. He grew very skillful. We traveled without incident, always keeping the main road on our left. There were immense fields of fig trees and forests of pines which mounted to the summits of the Sierra de Caballs, the ones the International Brigade had fought so hard for in July 1938. It was up there that they would look for us. In the valley, all along the road, there were far fewer Civil Guardsmen. All around were gardens with little houses, most often abandoned. The nights were cold, but not as cold as in the region of Zaragoza. We could treat ourselves to the pleasure of long naps under the trees. For us the important thing was to stay well rested. A tired man is less alert and lets himself be surprised. Our provisions were getting low. We ate what we could find. One afternoon I was able to kill a large snake. I skinned it and then grilled it. Everyone refused to eat it except the boy, who feasted with me. We had a good-sized piece left over that we kept for the next day.

In the early morning we met a peasant and his cart on the road. He was going to Asco to deliver sacks of flour. They were small sacks, a hundred pounds each. We took one and I gave the peasant a thousand pesetas. He offered us his lunch for the journey. I put it into my pack and offered him a package of cigarettes. We left with our sack. I saw a house a bit hidden in a garden. I sent in the boy. With him the people were less suspicious than with us. He could go anywhere. It was a young family with a small child. The husband was a road repairman. The house was rather large. Fernando explained that there were five of us. The man came back with the boy. He shook our hands and took us to the house.

When the wife saw the hundred-pound sack of flour she didn't look twice. They had no oven. But I found a large sheet of iron. We cleaned it well. My men didn't know that I had been a baker. My first care was to prepare the dough so that it would have time to rise. The boy with Vicente and Mier went out back to gather wood under the olive trees and get some pine branches. We didn't go outside. It was Sunday and many people were on the road going to the town of Asco, only six miles away. We had hidden our submachine guns in a cupboard but our pistols and daggers were still at our waists. The wife killed a chicken; the man went to the cellar to fetch a jug of wine. We each offered him a package of cigarettes. He didn't smoke, but he said he could exchange them for good things. Now the fire was burning well in the fireplace. On the sheet of iron I made round rolls, loaves wiped with oil, and, with a little sugar, milk and eggs, some round cakes. Everyone sat around drinking, watching me make the bread and kidding me. Everyone had to put his word in; they didn't know I used to be in the trade. I had made my dough by ten o'clock. Little Fernando was very helpful. He watched me make it. Like all children, he was interested in everything and had to touch it all.

The fire was going strong in the fireplace. I put on six medium-sized pieces of wood, two in the middle, the others on the ends. When they were burning well I placed the iron sheet on the grill and put my rolls on it. From time to time I stirred the ashes to keep up a good heat and now and then I added twigs of pine and olive. The first rolls were a little flat; the sheet had been too hot. But the others came out well rounded. The wife put them on a shelf in the cupboard as they were done. I made them in abundance, some to leave here, some to take along in our packs. Then I baked the cakes. It took three hours. We sat down at the table, ate and drank. What a sight to watch them all eating my rolls!

As night fell we prepared to leave. The repairman's wife wanted us to stay and rest several days. But that would be too dangerous for them: it would surely end with our being discovered. I gave them a thousand pesetas. I added two packages of cigarettes; the others each gave them one too. We filled our packs with rolls and cake. The woman gave us a bottle of olive oil. The boy had also filled his rucksack. The repairman put two cartons of milk in it.

When it was dark we slipped outside. We went across the fields. We crossed the railroad line and soon were in sight of the river Ebro, which we had to cross. We sneaked into the shelter of a large canefield and slept. At night the boy was always at my side. He had a good ear. At the slightest noise he touched my shoulder, most often for nothing.

At dawn I looked carefully all around. On the left there was a railroad bridge; it was surely guarded. At this time of year the water was high and the currents were rapid. On our right, about five hundred yards away, I saw four large boats moored on the bank. Softly, we advanced through the canes toward them. When we were in range I sent the boy to see if there were oars in them and if there was anyone around. The boy saw an old man. He asked him if for pay he would give us a boat ride for a bit of fishing. The old man said, "I'll go get the oars. They're in the shed and then we can go with your friends." While the boy was talking we had made the mistake of advancing to the bank. The shed was a hundred yards away; I sent Vicente to accompany the old man and the boy. The old man didn't want them to come with him. That disturbed me a bit. Then I gave the order to hide in the canes where we could watch the old man. When the three reached the shed, two Civil Guardsmen jumped out suddenly and seized Vicente by surprise. Meanwhile the old man pulled a pistol from his pocket and covered Fernando. I saw it all clearly through my binoculars, and the others could see them too with their naked eyes.

I had to decide at once. They were going to arrest Vicente or kill him on the spot. Then, in desperation, I decided: I would send Mier with Enrique back across the railroad; they would attack the shed from the rear. Mechol and I would advance to take the shed from the front. As we came close to the shed, the two Civil Guardsmen and the old man pushed their prisoners inside and went in with them. What should we do? Wait? Attack? Meanwhile Mier and Enrique had come up behind the shed. But on that side there was no window. There was only the door on our side. Time pressed; a reinforcement might arrive. I waited long minutes. Then I gave a cry of attack as loud as I could so our two friends would hear it inside. I threw a grenade just in front of the door; Mier threw another onto the roof. Then with a bound we were in the doorway. The Civil Guardsmen fired at us. I ducked and threw another grenade inside. We barely had time to get back behind the wall; the grenade exploded.

We went in again: it was a massacre. The two Civil

Guardsmen were lying mortally wounded; the old man was safe behind the fireplace. I killed him. Vicente was on the floor gravely wounded by bullets and shrapnel. Fernando was in the middle of the room, in pieces. He had taken the full force of the third grenade. I finished off the two Civil Guardsmen with my dagger. Then we left carrying Vicente, two by the shoulders and two by the legs. We put him into one of the boats. We ran back to the canefield to get our packs. Mier came running up with two pairs of oars and a plank. We pushed off, rowed a little to get some distance, then let the boat drift with the current.

I treated Vicente. He was covered with wounds and losing blood all over. He spoke little. He whispered in my ear, "When we came to the shed, the old man shouted to the Civil Guardsmen, 'It's the Reds!' and he pulled out his gun. He had Fernando in front of him. I couldn't shoot; if I had I would have killed the boy. Inside the shed, Fernando yelled at the Civil Guardsmen, 'You are all criminals. You killed my father and mother.' Then the Civil Guardsmen killed him." Vicente stopped speaking. He was crying. The tears rolled down his cheeks. I tried to comfort him as best I could.

Meanwhile the boat had reached the other side of the river. We got out. We wanted to carry Vicente, but it was impossible. The alert had been given on all sides; we would have to fight. So we put him in a thicket, placed a tommy gun in his hands, hurriedly embraced him one by one, and parted with regret. It was high time. Already they were shouting after us and bullets began flying close by. Moving guerrilla style we ran until we got to a large orchard. We hid behind a thick hedge. I looked for a landmark to get ready for the next dash. Then, my eyes at the binoculars, I looked back at the boat we had left, then at the thicket where we had hidden Vicente. I knew he had to die there. After a moment I saw a group of Civil Guardsmen and civilians approaching in the open. Vicente's tommy gun spat. He fired and fired. He cut down five. Two got up again, wounded. The others were dead. Then I heard a pistol shot. Vicente had shot himself.

I stayed a moment more, not knowing what to do. We were only four. But we had our packs full of bread, a quart of oil, ammunition, three grenades apiece, plenty of tobacco. One comrade lost or many — we were used to it. But today it was Vicente, my first lieutenant, lost because of my own mistake, and little Fernando, an innocent child. The four of us set off, heavy with sadness. We crossed the orchard and clambered up the hill. When we came to the top, I observed with the binoculars. Civil Guardsmen were mounting on both flanks. They intended to encircle us. So I applied my tactic.

To escape we were going to go down on the side where they were fewest. On the left they were coming in three groups; on the right they were all together. We would have to pass on the right. We descended and set up an ambush in an open space, lying behind some rocks. They thought we were in the cover of the woods; they would never dream we were in these rocks. I gave my orders: at the signal fire a burst, then one grenade each, because if by bad luck they had the advantage, we would need the other grenades for the finish. Don't try to collect weapons. We would save ourselves by climbing down to the left then climbing up again from behind to get the ones who escaped. Finally we would descend rapidly a short way and form another ambush to surprise any reinforcements who might come up.

The group approached. They climbed rifles in hand, but talking among themselves unsuspectingly. They were ten yards away. One of them saw me but he didn't have time to move. I fired bullet by bullet, grimacing. The others each swept a burst and threw their grenades. We came out, got behind them and finished them off. By luck none of our men had even been scratched. It was too bad there had been four civilians with the Civil Guardsmen, but undoubtedly they were Falangists or new Fascists.

We went back to the highway. In the distance I saw the power line. We were safe.

We walked all day and almost all night. We were tired; we had to find a hideout. We hid in a grove of hazelnut trees and slept, guarded by a sentinel. The highway wasn't far. We could hear the cars and trucks going by. In the morning I recognized the area. I had come to these hills for shooting exercises. We were close to Molerussa. There were caves in the hills. We found one which had three entrances, one high on the mountain and the other two at least thirty yards to the right and left. We were far from the road; we would be safe. We found empty crates with which we made tables and benches. With others we could make a fire. The dry wood wouldn't make much smoke. My friends kidded me a bit because we had nothing to cook. We dined on bread and hazelnuts.

In the afternoon I went out with Mier. We went down

to the highway. While he stood watch I cut the telephone wire, made some coils, and we went back up the mountain. We stopped under a pine and with the copper wire I made loops for snaring rabbits. I knew they would be everywhere at night. Then I cut stakes and showed Mier how to set up the snares, after rubbing the wire with weeds so it wouldn't have the smell of our hands. You had to place the loop at the height of a closed fist. For hares you added another thumb. We put sixty in the meadow and a hundred on the hillside. When we got back to the cave about three hours later, Mier told what we had done. The other two started to laugh and make fun of me. From time to time I went out to look at the sky. Finally they asked why I was doing that. I told them I was looking to see if there would be a moon or whether the sky would be overcast. When the weather is rainy the rabbit comes out just long enough to eat without going far. But if there is a fine moon, he plays, runs after the females, digs at the earth and goes all over. The Finn had taught me that when we were camping under the hazelnut trees, that Fourteenth of July when Commissar Tito got me drunk.

The night was clear. About eleven I awakened Mier. The others wanted to come along too to have a look. They took the packs and we went out. As soon as we came to the hill, they didn't want to go back. The rabbits scurried away as we advanced and were caught in the loops. In the meadow we filled a cape with them; there wasn't room for them all in our packs. While we collected the rabbits, I reset the snares, then we went back to the cave. We had taken seventy-two rabbits. About two we returned. This time I picked up the snares and

looped them over my arm. We counted sixty-one rabbits. That made a hundred thirty-three for the night.
We skinned four rabbits right away, one apiece, and
put them on the fire to cook. We had a feast. Afterward
we smoked as much as we wanted; we had plenty of
tobacco. We spent a good morning, then cooked twelve
rabbits, three for each of us, and wrapped them in paper
in our packs for the route. Afterwards I sent Mechol to
the village. He was to find the owner of a small restaurant I knew there. We stayed to survey the ap-
proaches in case he got a bad reception. After a while
he came back with two boys carrying sacks. So that the
boys wouldn't know where they had been taken, Antonio
and Mier went to the cave to get the crates of rabbits.
When they came back we dumped the rabbits into the
sacks and we all went back to the restaurant together.
The owner took us into a back room. We emptied the
sacks. The owner told me he was going to cook them
all and put them to marinate in jars. The restaurant
would have rabbit for a month. He gave us each a large
five-pound loaf of bread from a hidden supply he kept.
Also a large sausage apiece and ten or twelve pounds of
Spanish sausages. Then I offered him a large box of
cigars. He couldn't believe his eyes. He wanted to buy
all our tobacco. I told him we bought but we sold nothing, and I took a big roll of pesetas from my pocket. He
looked at us all, began to laugh and said, "And to think
in the village they say you were all killed when you
crossed the Ebro." I replied they had killed one of us
but we had killed many of them. Then he had the table
set for us and we all ate with his family. The dining
room nearby was full of workers, peasants passing

through, and even soldiers and three Civil Guardsmen eating in a small room at the side. The owner served us himself. While eating and drinking well we still kept on the alert. After the meal we drank cognac and smoked a cigar. The owner told us to stay until supper; he would give us a bedroom in the back with no risk. To be sure I sent one man into the garden for surveillance. The two boys stayed to talk with us. They had no work. They were nice but lacked experience. I gave them each five hundred pesetas. Evening came. We had supper with the whole family and in the clear night we returned to our cave.

The next day we left. On passing by the hill we found two more rabbits in traps I had missed. We put them in our jackets and went on, up and down the hills, without ever losing sight of our guiding thread, the power line. The slopes were well cultivated: olive trees, grapevines, hazelnut trees and carob trees. All around were lots of little farmhouses, and here and there on the slopes little villages. On the heights of the small mountains there were pines; brooks flowing down the slopes nourished the orchards and gave water to the villages. Peasants went to and from their work on all sides. They were a silent, stingy lot; they never had anything to share with you, but if you showed them money or tobacco they would sell their best friend.

We came to a high village called Torre de Fontaubella, where I had been two years before. I asked an old peasant who the mayor was.

He said, "The same one as in the time of the Republicans."

I said, "Then he is a traitor?"

He answered, "That's for sure. In the time of the Republicans he wouldn't let us have anything, neither wine nor oil. He said everything was for the army. But which army? We knew when the Francoists arrived. He got all his merchandise out and called them all patriots. So he was named mayor by the Nationalists."

I knew him well myself. During the war, when we had been camping under the hazelnut trees, I had gone to him for some wine and domestic rabbits; but he had said he could sell nothing without an order signed by the general staff in Barcelona. And now, the peasant said, it was the same way. He lived alone with all his merchandise refusing to sell or share anything.

We waited for night, then entered the village. Mechol and I went to the mayor's house. Antonio and Mier hid across the street awaiting orders. I knocked at the door. He opened; I asked for bread and wine. He said he had nothing here. I had eased little by little into the corridor and suddenly I pointed my submachine gun at him. Mechol had Antonio and Mier come in. They searched the villa; there was no one. In the cellar there were hundreds of bottles of wine and cans of food. Smoked hams hung in the granary with sacks of all kinds of dried vegetables. I had the packs filled up. In the office I found 22,480 pesetas and some packages of tobacco and cigarettes. The front door was well locked, there was no hurry. We would have supper. So we put everything out on the table, the best wines, a ham, bread and rolls, and we invited the mayor to eat with us. I had no intention of letting him live, but I had never tortured anyone or made anyone suffer. We ate well, but you couldn't say the mayor had very much appetite. We sat a long time tasting everything in the kitchen. Then I went into the office, tore the lid off a large cardboard box, and with a little stick dipped in ink wrote on the cardboard in big letters, THIS IS THE WAY TRAITORS TO THE REPUBLIC DIE, signed EL MEXICANO. We executed the mayor and put the sign on his chest.

We left loaded with provisions and went along following the crests of the hills. There was nothing but rocks and little shrubs, but there were old trenches which made good refuges. The third day I left our shelter at daybreak to look around through the binoculars. It was unbelievable! There were Civil Guardsmen on horseback on all sides. Two by two they were patrolling in all directions. It was lucky I had seen them. We went to hide in an old machine-gun post. I could survey the whole valley through the battlement. Two guardsmen with their horses came up to our position. They passed within five yards of us. They stopped, inspecting the horizon. We could hear them talking. Then they left, but they continued searching the hills the whole day. We didn't move. Two watched while two slept. We didn't leave until night.

We came to large mountains covered with pines. There we were safer. Suddenly we saw the sea shining in the moonlight. Now we would cut to the left. We couldn't get lost; by following the coast we would come to France.

Soon we descended to the fields. Before being freed, my friend the Catalan wood merchant had made me a map of the region and I wanted to go and see him at his village. We arrived there at night. My friend's house was across from the Civil Guard barracks.

I found it easily, had my men hide in a demolished house and went to knock on the door of the wood merchant. He embraced me with joy and took me inside. I told him my whole story. Then he went with me to get my friends, and we all went back with him to a large courtyard behind the house. He had us climb into the granary and settled us in a garret where there were all kinds of old things. From the window we could see the street and the hill of pines over the rooftops. We had nothing to fear. He was very friendly with the captain of the Civil Guard. We ate with the family and then climbed back up to sleep. My friend had brought two old mattresses. We passed a good night. The next day we bathed and shaved. We had to be presentable for our arrival in Barcelona, which was not far away. We stayed three days to rest up well.

As far as my friend knew, the Civil Guard did not go into the mountains. They patrolled the highway and the entrances and exits of the villages. The most dangerous part for us would be getting across Barcelona. He explained the route to me carefully. We left in the evening. The moon was as bright as day. I didn't give my friend money as he was stinking with money, merchandise and farmhouses. He was one of the richest men in the village, but he had remained a good Republican.

We were going by way of the mountains. There was nothing but gorges and ravines. We had to creep up and down, at times to advance only a hundred yards. But the highway was dangerous: it wound back and forth, and in the places you least expected them military trucks and Civil Guard patrols in cars could appear. We walked many days like that without incident. We saw the sea again and followed it from afar. One evening we were following a trail worn in the side of a mountain of pines. There were caves fixed up as houses, but they had all been abandoned. But in one we found a family anyway. There were two women, two children, an old man and a rather tired man of about fifty. We went in. They were so poor they didn't even have a piece of bread to offer us. I asked them what they ate. They showed me a pot full of dried-up carrots and a basket of wild apples. Sometimes they went down to the sea and gathered mussels and fish. They had no furniture, nothing but crates. But there was no shortage of wood and they had a good fire. They said the Civil Guard came by every two days and searched to see if they had hidden any arms. We spent the night sleeping in the straw with them. In the morning I gave them some bread, six red sausages, a packet of tobacco and a thousand pesetas. They were happy.

We left and a little farther on we climbed down the rocks to the sea. Mechol the Galician had no fear of cold water. He undressed and plunged in. He collected mussels big as a fist and quantities of oysters. Meanwhile the rest of us collected crabs. We climbed back up to the mountain. In a clearing we made a fire with dry wood and put the crabs in to roast. We ate the oysters and mussels with vinegar. We boiled the leftover ones in a can, put them in a well-folded rag, and left — just in time. Once we were on the path we saw two Civil Guardsmen climbing up towards us, followed by a forest guard carrying a shotgun, his cartridge pouch at the waist and a large rucksack on his back. We set up an ambush and killed all of them before they could make a move. We took the Civil Guardsmen's ammunition. In the forester's rucksack we found a large loaf of bread, a bar of chocolate, two partridges and a wild rabbit. We took it all including the shotgun and cartridges.

We climbed a bit higher up the mountain, but kept within sight of the sea. We found trenches and bunkers and even caves. We stopped in one of them. There we could make a fire without danger. We roasted the rabbit and the two partridges and ate some wild apples for dessert. We smoked a big cigar and settled down for the night.

The next day we went down to get closer to the coast. By the sea there was only a wide beach which followed the coast. In the distance we could see the high mountains. Through here there were only well-cultivated hills with roads and farmhouses all around and a highway skirting the beach. Many people moved about. Fortunately it was winter; the beaches were deserted. We advanced prudently, by paths and little roads, walking one by one ten yards apart, our weapons hidden under our jackets or capes. Only Antonio carried the shotgun on his arm like a hunter. In the evening we saw the lights of Barcelona and the big ships anchored in the harbor.

We spent the night in a hut. In the morning we had to find a way to cross the city. We started out and found a highway which brought us to the first houses in the outlying quarters of the city. I noticed one house, a large one, with a courtyard and barns. We slipped into one of them: it was full of vegetables. In the courtyard there were lots of people loading and unloading merchandise vans. I left Mechol and Mier in the barn with our packs and went into the courtyard with Antonio. I asked for the boss. An employee led us to an office at the house. The boss looked a bit askance at us. Audacity was our only hope. I told him I had to go to Mataró, beyond Barcelona, and I would pay well for a truck to take us and our merchandise. He hesitated. Then I asked him to send the employee away and when he had gone out I told him who I was, why I was in Barcelona and what I wanted to do now. I said he would drive us to Mataró himself and if he refused he was a dead man. Then he smiled and told me to keep cool: he would drive us himself in his car as the trucks were usually searched. Then I sent Antonio to get the two others. The boss had a good snack made for us: fried eggs with ham and a good bottle of wine. He talked to us about the war. I believed we could trust him, but I signaled to Antonio not to let him out of his sight. He had our canteens filled with wine and lots of things put in our packs. I gave him fifteen thousand pesetas and two boxes of big cigars. He ordered his employee to put two cases of dried fruits and some packages of onions and garlic into the car. We got in. He was a bit surprised to see four submachine guns. To impress him even more I showed him the rucksack of grenades. I forgot to say that during these preparations Mechol and Mier were laughing at a little monkey jumping around in a big cage by the boss's door. They had never seen anything like that in their lives.

When we were in Barcelona I asked to go down the Calle Tallere. I wanted to say hello to Antonio Palmerón, an old comrade from the camp at Miranda. I quickly went up to his room with a case of figs and dates and the packages of garlic and onions. He was very happy to see me. I gave him fifteen thousand pesetas as it was easy to see he wasn't very rich, and three packages of cigarettes. Then we left. It was just as it had been two years before. We crossed the Plaza de Colón, passed in front of the large pillar, went down by the port and took the road to Mataró. There was nothing but factories. A little before Mataró, I had our driver take a road leading to the mountains. When we came to the forest, we got out.

The Border

WE CLIMBED through the forest. Everything was calm. We only met some people gathering wood. When we got high up we saw the high mountains in the distance with their snow-covered peaks. We descended to cross the railroad. It went to France along the coast, but you couldn't cross the border that way. To escape from Nationalist Spain you had to cross over the mountains. By following the flank of the mountains always keeping to the north, the railroad would be on the left. It was the one leading up to Puigcerdá, the same one I had taken when I came from France. There was no danger of getting lost.

As we climbed again we saw a large château, maybe the one belonging to my old commandant. Through the binoculars I saw lots of civilians going in and out. We made a detour and afterwards came back into the forest. It was pleasant. We had plenty of cold food and there was good spring water, as well as nuts and rather over-ripe wild apples. I had divided the bread into four rations for four days. We wouldn't have to pass through the villages. We walked and walked and still didn't progress very far: we had to follow the railroad from a distance and that meant going up and down all the time. The nights were cold. When we could, we slept in abandoned farms or shepherds' cottages, but only when we were near a village, as the Civil Guardsmen patrolled in the mountains. The farther we went the more surveillance posts there were. Sometimes we had to sleep in the forest; we squeezed together in the shelter of a rock and woke up in the morning all numb.

We came in view of Vich, a town known for its sausages. There was lots of traffic in the valley, many military trucks on the roads. We kept going up through the forest. We came on a river, the Ter, which flows by Gerona. There was no way to cross it so we followed it until we came to a little plank bridge used by the peasants. We climbed again and came to a main road that I recognized. It led to Olot passing by a mountain with a church on top.

The road climbed to the right. We followed it to the top and came in sight of an old village perched on a hill. On the road below it there was a Civil Guard post. We had almost finished our provisions; there were only two cans, some tobacco, and oil and vinegar left. Rather than ask the timid peasants, we would go and take some food from the Civil Guardsmen, who surely had plenty of everything.

We waited for night. We went down to the road.

Everything was quiet. The windows of the little building were lighted. We approached softly: four Civil Guardsmen were eating supper at a table. We threw a grenade through a windowpane then kicked open the door and fired a burst. Mechol watched the rear of the building and Antonio the front from behind a tree. I went in with Mier. Two guardsmen were dead. I finished off the third, who was badly wounded. The fourth was in a side room; we killed him. Now we were masters of the post. These bastards had enough food for a week. While Mier filled the rucksacks I looked at the papers. I found in a drawer a list of about a hundred suspects from the region. I put the list in a sack. We took the clips and three boxes of bullets, a ten-liter demijohn of wine, and started climbing to get back to the heights before daylight. It was tiring as we were so heavily loaded.

We came to a clearing from which we had a good view for observing, and there was a thick bush against a rock where we could hide if it was necessary. We rested in the shelter of the rock. At dawn I looked with the binoculars in the direction of the little building. There were already two trucks full of soldiers and Civil Guardsmen. They wouldn't wait long to start looking for us. We ate some of everything, drank some wine from the demijohn and filled our canteens with the rest. Then we carefully cleaned our guns and made a burrow like foxes in the ground under the big bush. The men crawled inside with the rucksacks. I covered up the entrance to the burrow and put a small dead tree on top. While the others slept I stayed to watch through the branches. The trucks left during the morning. We spent the day and night in our hiding place. In the morning we set off again.

We went slowly and cautiously. We came to the foot of a mountain that was all rock and no trees. If we were spotted there they wouldn't take long to catch us. So we went around it, always staying under the trees.

In the afternoon we came on a post, or rather a bunker, as we could see the barrel of a machine gun or automatic rifle. There were three gunners sitting quietly in their shirt sleeves enjoying the sun. We advanced silently to a distance of ten yards. We had to prevent them from getting back into the post. We fired our bursts together. One of them crawled toward the door. I threw a grenade, which fell on top of him. Then we went inside. The bunker was made of thick concrete. It commanded the entire valley; at the bottom was the railroad. There was quite an arsenal in a little tunnel carved in the side of the mountain, cases of ammunition, excellent pineapple grenades, mortars and shells, cases of new rifles and sticks of dynamite. We took four modern automatics with five clips, a box of bullets and four grenades apiece. We filled a pack with dynamite, a box of detonators, a roll of slow fuse and another of fast. We left our tommy guns. Then we put a packet of dynamite in a case of grenades, emptied a can of oil over it, stuck in a wick and detonator, lit it and left in a hurry. We weren't three hundred yards off when it blew. We missed being killed by the flying rock; fortunately we were lying against the slope of a ravine and the rocks flew over us. When we got up the forest was on fire. We quickly got to the top of the mountain. We were tired but had to use all our energy to get farther away. At last we came to an abandoned house. It had two huge fig trees on either side of the door and a little garden in back. We settled in for a good rest. When night came the sky was red from the fire. We heard trucks passing on the road in the valley. We slept well in our shelter, under the guard of a sentinel changed every two hours. At dawn we got up feeling fresh.

We had to prevent reinforcements from arriving. We went down to the road and followed along it, keeping under cover. We came to a stream which the road crossed by a wooden bridge. We watched it awhile through the binoculars; it was not guarded. We went down and put four sticks of dynamite under the beams, with two detonators and five yards of slow fuse. We lit it and left to stash ourselves in a ravine up above. The fuse was slower than I thought; we waited half an hour. Then the bridge blew up. It was a complete success — no vehicle could pass.

We went on by short stages, taking it easy, watching and listening. Any path could bring danger, and it wasn't long before we found it. All at once we were in view of a farm about a hundred yards below. As I was taking out my binoculars soldiers poured out of it and began shooting up at us with a machine gun. We ran to get to the other slope of the mountain. The soldiers were sure to chase us. When we got to the top I observed the enemy's movements with the binoculars. One group was climbing up right in front of us, the other was going around the side of the mountain. We went down to try to pass behind the second group. We made it by about fifty yards. They were some thirty soldiers and almost as many officers. When they were at the top, we were at the bottom. We crossed the river, which wasn't deep, and started up the side of the next mountain. It was less wooded, with fields cultivated in terraces. Lots of fruit trees, but no more fruit. Many stone huts. We made our halts to rest and from time to time met peasants working in the fields. They were timid, afraid to speak. If we stopped to say a few words they kept looking all around, muttering that the Civil Guardsmen were everywhere.

Now we were above a valley with a road and railroad running through. I remembered it well. Olot was a few miles on the left, the village of Las Presas on the right. In the distance I could see the church in front of which we had got onto the trucks that took us to the station in Olot. Two hundred yards further down was the farm where I lived a month when our commando unit of the XVth Brigade was formed. I watched through the binoculars. There were soldiers in the village but not at the farm. We hid in a thicket and waited for nightfall. Then we advanced toward the farm, slipping from one bush to the next. When we were close to the farm we waited. After a while a woman came out to empty a pail in the courtyard almost in front of us. I called softly, "Amelia." She stopped, surprised. I came out of the straw; she recognized me at once. "Oh, Paco!" She took me by the hand and made me go into the house. When the door was closed she let go of the pail and fell on me in tears. She couldn't speak, she just kept saying, "Oh, Paco! Oh, Paco!" After a while she told me her father and brother had been shot and her mother had died from grief. Her sister was married in Barcelona. She had stayed on with her grandfather and two young boys who took care of the cows. The farm sheds were used as warehouses by the engineers who were putting barbed wire around Olot and up into the mountains to prevent escapes into France. All day long the soldiers came and went with their material. I would have to stay hidden in the daytime. The soldiers slept in the village and the Civil Guardsmen never came to the farm as it was occupied by the army.

I went to get my comrades. We drank milk and ate dried beans with potatoes and a little piece of bread. We made a hideout in a cellar. The boys brought fresh hay. We stayed there and slept for three days. We came out in the evening when the soldiers had left. The first night Amelia heated huge tubs of water. We had a good bath and Amelia washed all our clothes. We sat by the fireplace and ate chestnuts. Amelia laughed at my prison stories. But afterwards she cried and kept saying, "Oh, Paco! They'll kill you too." She said that if bad weather overtook us in the mountains we would die of cold, that the cold on the French side was terrible, that we would have to stay hidden here and wait for the thaw. I told her that the bad weather would help us, that in the good season there were soldiers and Civil Guardsmen everywhere, even at night, and that if you remained hidden you were always caught. You had to keep moving to escape the enemy. We left the fourth night. Amelia gave us a loaf of bread each, some sausages and boiled potatoes. I left her ten thousand pesetas.

I knew the country well. These were the mountains where we had practiced climbing rocks, crossing rivers, blowing up old houses to learn to handle explosives, and getting through barbed wire. We left for the mountains to rejoin the railroad to Puigcerdá, avoiding Olot, which according to Amelia was full of soldiers. We came on a large shed surrounded by barbed wire. There were piles of planks all around. The night was clear; I walked around the shed observing it carefully. It was not guarded. We slipped under the barbed wire. Above the door was a sign saying it was a workshop of the army engineers. We approached. I looked inside through a wire window. I cut the wire to see better. It was a large carpentry shop. I went in. There were thirty workbenches, machines, piles of planks and new benches, windows and doors. On the wall at the back was a picture of Franco as big as life. That made me mad as it reminded me of all the times I had to salute that picture with my arm upraised, and of how you were slapped when you forgot and had to stand in front of it at attention for an hour. Then I got the idea that this workshop could help us escape, by attracting the attention of the troops and the Civil Guardsmen. I called two of the men inside while the others stood guard. We poured cans of oil, gasoline and paint on the piles of shavings and all around the workshop. I put sticks of dynamite between the gasoline cans, set a fuse, lit it, and we left in the direction of the railroad. When we came to the forest on the mountain facing it, it exploded. What a fire! You could see as plain as in daylight. A little later, with my binoculars I could see soldiers coming from everywhere towards the fire. We continued to climb through the forest. All at once we saw some Civil Guardsmen coming down on the run. We made an ambush. We had heard many explosions as we were climbing. The Civil Guardsmen ran with their rifles in hand but without precaution. We killed all seven. A little farther on we saw some soldiers coming down. We let them pass. Then we came out of the forest. We had to climb from rock to rock. Day broke. Below we could see an anthill of soldiers and Civil Guardsmen. When we came to a cover of oak trees, we rested in the shelter of a bush. We heard a plane and I watched it with the binoculars. It flew along the edge of the mountains making circles. Twice it dived to strafe a path a little below us.

When the plane was gone we went down to the path. It ended in a small gorge and there we found two civilians killed and another wounded in the arm. He had no weapons. I spoke to him. He said he was trying to get to France with a companion. They had had a guide but now he was dead. I treated his wound and took out a bullet which had only gone into the muscle. He said his name was Luis Quamara, from Granada, and he had been a political commissar. When his dressing was finished he came with us. But he was tired. Walking slowly we had time to enjoy the landscape. We came in view of the high mountains covered with snow. How beautiful they were! Then all of a sudden there was a lake shining at our feet. It was surrounded by forest except on our side, where the rocky side of the mountain dropped down. There were at least two miles to cover in the open before we came to the lake and its forest. I looked all around a long time with the binoculars. Then we crossed as fast as we could. I was not afraid of the airplanes. We were lucky; we got to the lake, went into the trees and drank the good water. The forest was thick. There was nothing to fear, but as we couldn't see the sky I had to climb to the top of a tree from time to time to check our route. We flushed hares and stags. When the wind was against us we got within ten yards

of the stags. We managed to kill a doe. We roasted it,
ate well and had enough meat left for many days. It
would keep in this cold. I noticed a certain kind of grass
that sprang up again right away without leaving a trace
when the stags jumped over it. I tried running on it; it
sprang up behind me. That was good to know for covering our trail. We advanced under the big trees. It was
cold and raw. We finally came to a main road and got
a nasty surprise: we were hardly five hundred yards
from Olot. We had gone in a big circle. We hid in a
cave, rested all day and night, then set off for the mountains again in the morning.

We'd only gone a mile when we met a civilian who
looked like a fugitive; torn clothes, dirty and unshaven,
bad shoes. He was unarmed. He spoke Castilian and I
questioned him. He said he was trying to get to France
and was here because he had an aunt in Olot who was
able to help him. I was surprised to see him leaving his
relative in such miserable condition. We always left
clean after staying with people who sheltered us. I
asked him where his aunt lived and he described a brick
villa below the road near the edge of the town. He
showed me his papers; his name was Márquez Sánchez
Olivar. I sensed that something was wrong. I changed
my plan and decided to go back to the cave. I left my
two new companions there guarded by Mier and Mechol
and went down towards Olot with Antonio. We were
careful to avoid meeting the patrol. I knew the town
well and it didn't take long to find the aunt's villa. An
old woman opened the door and we went in. I told her
not to be afraid, that I had lived in Olot as a Republican
soldier, that I was going to France and wanted to buy

provisions. She took us to the kitchen. An old man was there and a sweet girl of about ten. The old woman gave us all the bread in the house, a black sausage, a big cheese, and filled our canteens with wine. There were some photos on the commode; one of them was a man dressed as a Falangist. I recognized my Márquez. I asked who he was. The old man said it was one of their nephews, a bad young man in the secret police who tried to trap unfortunates like us trying to cross the border. He had had many arrested. The old woman told me he had even had her husband arrested and put in a concentration camp. They were afraid of him but he made them give the impression of being on his side by displaying his picture with the other family photos. I asked his name. The old woman said it was Vicente Puch but he had false papers. She told me to be careful to avoid him, he was in the region and he deceived people by appealing for pity and afterward he had them arrested and they were killed on the spot. I thanked her, gave her three thousand pesetas and gave the old man all the cigarettes I had on me.

We went back to the cave. I told Antonio not to tell the others what we had heard. We divided the provisions, giving each his share as though everything was all right, and left again for the mountains.

Once more we climbed up through the forest. We were going to try going around the mountain so we wouldn't come back to the lake. As night fell we emerged on a small road. We walked parallel to it, at a short distance. After a bit it turned and crossed a small stream over a wooden bridge. I observed carefully; the bridge wasn't guarded. We crossed it and a mile further on there was a small farm. I knocked at the door. An old woman opened it. In the room were an old man and three young children. They were very poor. They had a goat and a few chickens. The old man told me they made their living raising rabbits. They had hundreds in cages. He offered me supper. I told him I had friends with me, but I would buy rabbits and pay well. We ate with them the little they had: boiled potatoes and chestnuts. After supper the old woman got up to put the children to bed. We stayed by the fire talking with the old man. He said that a mile from the path there was a Civil Guard post on the road leading to the pass. The guardsmen never came by here. They patrolled the road to Ripoll. He had seen them today leading three prisoners. It was the pass they watched. If you wanted to escape you had to go over the top of the mountain. I said we would rest by the fire and leave at dawn. Then I made a sign to Mechol and went out to inspect the surroundings.

This time I had a traitor with me! It was necessary to unmask him, but skillfully. Behind the house there was a big pile of vine branches for firewood and also a pile of stumps. We used some to make a hiding place. Then I told Mechol to go in and tell the others to sleep by the fire, I would mount the first guard. Two hours later I went in and woke Márquez and told him it was his turn to stand guard. I went out with him and posted him at the beginning of the path leading down to the Civil Guard post by the road, telling him to keep a close watch for any patrol coming up to the farm. I went back to the house, awakened my companions and led them to the hiding place. Then I made a detour and posted myself halfway down the path leading to the road. At the end of a half hour I heard my man coming down. He passed so close I could have touched him. I leapt up, thrust my knife in his heart, threw him to the ground and cut his throat. Then I took out a piece of paper on which I'd written: *This is how traitors die,* and I put it on his chest with a rock on top of it.

Then I went back to the farm. I woke up our friends and told them what happened. We were going to attack the Civil Guard post where the old man said the prisoners were being held waiting to be transferred to Barcelona. I took two big rabbits, killed them and put them in my rucksack. I woke up the old man and gave him a thousand pesetas and a package of tobacco. Then we went down towards the road.

It was like the post at Vich. The guardsmen were eating at the table. We made the usual attack: grenades through the window and bursts of gunfire through the open door. While Mier and Mechol cleaned up below I bounded upstairs and killed three guardsmen who were trying to get away. I heard the prisoners shouting behind a door at the end of the corridor. I went down again. Mier and Mechol had finished their task. They had killed a lieutenant hiding under a desk in the office. We tore out the telephone cord and each man did his job. I took the keys I found hanging on a wooden rack and hurriedly freed the prisoners. There were four of them. We came down just as there was a burst of machine-gun fire on the road. I ran to the window and jumped out. I saw Luis coming toward me laughing so hard he couldn't stop. He couldn't speak, he was so overcome. Finally the words poured out: a Civil Guardsman had been able to hide as we went in. Luis had been watching and saw him come out through a window and start running toward the village. He let him run a moment and then machine-gunned him. It was the first Civil Guardsman he himself had killed; that's why he was laughing so hard. We rejoined the others who were waiting under the trees. One of the prisoners, an old man, could barely walk. He was from a nearby village. I told him to try to get to his house and hide there. The other three came with us. We climbed rapidly back up the mountain. At the first halt we counted up. We had killed nine Civil Guardsmen, one of them a lieutenant, and one traitor. We captured two tommy guns and thirty grenades that Mier had wrapped in a shirt. We also had three new recruits, all Catalans. The youngest, Malaguez, was from Figueras. He knew the region well and would serve as our guide. The other two were called Ruissol and Castel. They were surely not traitors. They had been scheduled for the concentration camp and all three wanted nothing better than to join us in escaping to France. That had been their own intention. They had been taken by surprise with no weapons to defend themselves. Malaguez explained that we couldn't continue in the direction of the Aras pass. The border was hardly twenty-five miles away, but that was where it was guarded the most. In winter everybody who tried to get to France went that way because the mountains weren't so high. There were four passes but all were well guarded. Only smugglers could get through, often by paying the guards. It was better to follow the road and cross by Puigcerdá. It was three days' march, but we could follow the main road and the railroad from above. We couldn't get lost and we could always go down to one of the villages for provisions. We would have to keep our strength up with good nourishment to get through the cold and snow of the mountains.

Seeing the goal so near put us all in high spirits. We advanced easily through a forest covered with a light layer of snow. Unfortunately, when we had heard Luis's tommy gun we had all run out of the guard post and forgotten to take provisions. But I showed the others how to eat roots: you peeled them and then chewed on them a long time; a bitter but very nourishing juice came out. We had the luck to find a young wild boar. We roasted it and the eight of us finished it in one meal. We were not progressing very fast as our three new recruits were tired. The third day we went down to the valley to cross the highway and railroad. Climbing up again we came on a charcoal maker's hut. We slept there and spent the day resting. There was a good spring nearby. From time to time deer and stags came by, but our guide didn't want us to shoot so close to the road. The next morning I observed through the binoculars. Far behind us I saw a column of soldiers advancing as if they were following our tracks in the snow. They had three mules. We set off without hurry and kept under the cover of the trees. Then there was no more forest, only a huge bare mountain. It would be easy to surprise them there. Towards evening they stopped and put up their tents. They lit a fire. When night came we went back down towards them, making a detour to the side; guided by their fire, we came up behind them. They weren't two hundred yards away. I counted sixteen soldiers surrounded by six Civil Guardsmen. They had two machine guns on our side and two mortars in front, but the gunners weren't at their posts. There was a sentinel by the mortars. We heard the soldiers talking and laughing around the fire. The Civil Guardsmen were on one side eating. We could approach and surprise them with grenades. One soldier started to sing. He didn't sing "Cara al Sol"; it was an Andalusian song. He got up and started to dance. Through the binoculars I could see him snapping his fingers and the others seated in a circle clapped their hands. Luis, the political commissar, wanted us to attack. I said that I didn't kill soldiers. He baited me and I told him he didn't know everything I'd done, I had killed more than my share of enemies since I escaped. I was tired of killing. We had fought like good Republicans. We had avenged our dead comrades. Now we could get away to France, so we stayed there watching, and waited for them to leave.

In the morning they packed up their camp and went back towards the village we had seen the previous evening. We went over to the place where they had camped. We found a few potatoes and a sack of carob beans. We ate them all and set off. We found the forest again and when we came to the top of the mountain we saw an old village. Our guide said it was half abandoned and served as a station for smugglers. I observed carefully, then entered the village with Malaguez and Antonio. We went into a large house. I saw right away that we could buy a bit of everything, food and tobacco. The owner and his wife were old people. They understood right away where we were going. The owner invited me to go upstairs. Through a window he showed me a mountain all white with snow. He told me on the other side was France. At the bottom there was the railroad and the road which climbed Puerto de Tosas at about six thousand feet. But we couldn't get through that way. There were little concrete fortresses with machine guns guarding the passes and patrols of Civil Guardsmen everywhere. You had to pass over the ridges, but in winter it was dangerous. Once you were over the summits, you came down over Puigcerdá. The railroad went through the pass by a long tunnel, after which there were many small tunnels. The road went over the mountain. You had to cross the road, climbing through the forest. Two miles more and you were in France. The Civil Guardsmen never came here to the village at night because of the smugglers who attacked them.

I sent for the others. We ate a lot: ham, cold meat, wine and as much bread as we wanted. I had our packs filled with a little of everything and gave the man ten thousand pesetas. We spent the night in three bedrooms well heated by fireplaces. We stayed the next day to rest, and another night. We left at dawn, in the direction of the mountain of snow. Climbing steadily in snow is painful; we progressed very slowly. There were no traces of human beings, but we did see troops of wild goats. They were small, all white and had long goatees. There was always one perched on a pointed rock, his four feet together, watching while the others pawed the snow looking for food. Then we came to a pine forest half buried in snow. We saw very pretty chamois goats with little horns who didn't let us come close as the others did. They were also faster. There were lots of wild boars and some foxes, but no traces of humanity. We were still climbing. The trees were more scarce. When we arrived at the ridge we were struck by the wind and flurries of snow. Soon the blizzard was so heavy you couldn't see ten yards ahead. The whirling snow made us turn our heads. We didn't know where we were going; we had to stop.*

We each got behind a tree trunk. They were too small to give us much protection from the wind biting our faces. Our feet were in the most danger: I told everyone to make a hole in the snow and poke his feet in it. Then we put a blanket over our heads and there was nothing more to do but wait. The storm lasted two days and we stayed there shaking with cold. Towards the end we couldn't think straight. We dozed all the time. The morning of the third day the snow stopped falling. I shook the men to go on. Ruissol and Mechol had died from the cold. Luis had both feet frozen and couldn't walk. We made a stretcher with branches and went on, taking turns carrying him. We dragged on, weakened as we were from fatigue and hunger. At last we saw some smoke; it was a large farm covered with snow. The peasants made us drink a hot soup right away and when we were warmed up we went to sleep next to the cows. We rested three days and nights to regain our strength. The peasants cared for Luis, whose feet were all blue. They said he had to get to a doctor or he would lose his legs. We left still carrying him. Puigcerdá wasn't far. A fine snow was falling.

On leaving the forest we saw the railroad with all its

---

*Francisco must have been crossing the Sierra del Cadí, the summit of which is over 8,000 feet — and this at the end of January of 1941, one of the coldest winters that Europe had known in a long time. V. G.

tunnels. Beside the track there was a little house like the ones they have beside the routes for the workers. We were so cold we didn't hesitate to get a moment of shelter there and even make a fire in a small fireplace with a stack of wood by it. It felt so good to be warm again. But my mind was so numb from the cold that I forgot to post a sentinel outside. We thought of nothing but getting a bit of warmth as it had been so cold on top of the mountain that it was as though the cold had stayed in the marrow of our bones, in spite of the three days we passed in the good heat from the cows.

We left, following the railroad and looking for a passage where we could climb up to the road. We hadn't gone a hundred yards when from behind the embankment they hit us almost point-blank with tommy guns and grenades. Castel, Mier and Malaguez were killed at once, as was Luis on his stretcher. I managed to jump to the other side and Antonio was able to do the same, but he got a bullet in the shoulder. We sneaked along the embankment and got behind them. We had lost everything but my revolver and two grenades I had in my pockets. Antonio had his revolver but neither bullets nor grenades. They followed our tracks, shooting from a distance when they saw us. Detouring around the railroad we came to a small tunnel. Beside it the forest ran down to the track. I decided it was all or nothing. We went back a little to a turn of the track and hid in the brush. I gave Antonio a clip and one of my grenades. He was losing blood but could still move his arm. In a moment four Civil Guardsmen came running down the track. We let them approach, then we each threw our grenade and jumped out of the brush attacking them with our revolvers. All four guardsmen were dead. We took their clips and I took a tommy gun and two grenades. We ran toward the tunnel. It was less than fifty yards long. At the other end there was no one. The snow was falling heavily now. We hoisted ourselves up the slope and made it to the road. The snow fell heavier and heavier. They couldn't see us now, or even follow our footprints. I remembered what the old man had said: after the little tunnels, leave the road and climb straight ahead. Following the bank of the road I found the start of a little path. We took it. But now there were squalls of snow like the ones at the top of the mountain. I couldn't even see Antonio. Suddenly I stumbled into a deep crevasse. It was full of snow and I sank in up to my shoulders. I shouted for Antonio. I heard nothing, and I felt myself sinking. Finally the sounds wouldn't come out of my throat. I was about to die. I felt the cold mounting and little by little I couldn't even move my arms. Then I heard a voice calling me from above and I couldn't even respond. But I saw they had thrown a plank across and a man lowered himself down on a rope. He put it under my arms and from above the others pulled me up. A man put me over his shoulder. There was a house twenty yards away, all buried in the snow.

Inside there were lots of people. They laid me on the floor but not in front of the fire. An old woman and two old men removed my weapons, then undressed me and left me completely naked on the floor in front of all these women I didn't know. Then, in little dips, one of the men threw hot water all over my body. Then the one on the other side did the same with cold water. The first one started with the hot water again. They did that a good while, then raised me up, gave me a good rub-down, wrapped me in a heated blanket and put me by the hearth where a big fire was burning. I only looked and listened as I still couldn't talk. I stayed like that for three days, always seated by the fire, well nourished with bowls of milk and thick soups, but still without being able to speak and not thinking of anything. The cold that froze my tongue was still inside me.

I looked at the people. Because of the cold they all stayed in the house. There was an old woman who was always looking after me, five men, four women and two children between ten and fourteen. Two cast-iron pots hung over the fire. One was the animals' food, the other the people's. It was always the same: potatoes, chick-peas, and beans with a big chunk of pork. That made a rich soup that they ate in big brown pottery bowls, all at the same table. The master got the wine from a cup-board for which he had the key. He served a glass or half glass to each one depending on whether it was a man or a woman. After dinner the women sewed or knitted and the men sorted the corn, beans and chick-peas to put aside the seed grains. The women made fresh noodles: they kneaded the flour with eggs in big bowls, then worked the dough over the edge of the table. They left it under a cloth for a bit, then rolled vigorously on the table with their hands and the dough came off the edge like chips of wood. After that they put them in the pot where the soup was cooking. Everyone slept in the big room. There were no beds. They put up planks which were held on edge with their ends stuck into grooves in the wall, and threw good hay between them. Each person put a blanket over his section, lay down on it, put another blanket on top, and slept. In the morning the boys sorted out the clean hay. The rest was given to the animals.

But most of the day the men were bored. They played a bit of cards. None of them knew how to read. As soon as I found my tongue and my movements again, they were happy. I sat with them sorting corn and told about the war. Afterward the oldest ones told stories of their youth at a time when there was still a king in Spain.

They kept all the animals in the house. The cows were in a stable which opened onto the kitchen. Chickens, ducks and geese ran all around. These peasants had never worked for commercial purposes. They made their bread and had provisions for the entire year. They only sold what they had too much of, to buy what they were lacking. They had a big shed full of wood for the whole winter. They put unsplit tree trunks in the fireplace. They threw all the excrement out a window. That made a good dunghill below, which they collected in the springtime. It was while opening the window to throw out garbage that one of the women had heard my cries.

One evening I took out of my pocket the little sack where I kept my block of cigarette paper. It was the one I wrote my addresses and my accounts on. They were astonished when they saw me write. All were illiterate. The children watched me with curiosity. So I took a piece of a box and charcoal, drew the letters of the alphabet and taught them to read them. Then all the women came over, and the young men too. The next day they all begged for a lesson. I took a leather apron and hung it on the wall with two nails. It was like a blackboard, and I wrote the word "mama" and made the children spell it and the women repeat it. Word got around the whole village that there was a teacher giving a class. It wasn't a real village with a mayor and church, but just a few houses hanging on the mountainside. The next day all the parents came with their children. The kitchen was full of people. So I cut pieces of boxes and gave one to each child. Then I put little ends of burned wood in a pot. Each child seated along the table took one and drew the letter I wrote on the leather apron. At the end of three days they all spelled together. It made a noise like a real class. But when I taught them to count, the men and women wanted to learn too. In the evening after supper I was invited to come to other houses. There I taught the women to count money. I played the merchant across the table and they pretended they were buying. I took the money and taught them to read the figures on the bills and coins. They were happy.

I stayed more than fifteen days. They all wanted me to stay until spring. But it would have been stupid to get caught when I could practically touch the border. But they said with this cold even the smugglers weren't crossing. They hadn't seen it freeze so hard for twenty-five years. Anyone caught at night in the mountains would freeze to death for sure. The customs agents and even the Civil Guardsmen were staying by the fire that winter.

One day a doctor came up from Puigcerdá to see a sick man in danger of dying. He took the opportunity to examine the children. I was afraid one of them might mention the new teacher. So I decided to leave. The peasants gave me my weapons which they had hidden in the hay: my revolver with two clips and two grenades.

In a small rucksack they put a round bread, lots of ham, a red sausage and an onion. I left them all my money, forty-two thousand pesetas.

A little before night I left with the youngest of the men. We crossed a small river by sliding over the ice and then came in view of a village. I was in France.

I went into a bakery and told the woman I was a Frenchman who had escaped from the prisons of Spain. I gave her my revolver, the clips and the two grenades. I took off my legionnaire's greatcoat. She gave me some old civilian clothes and three thousand francs. Then she showed me how to get to the main road to Prades.

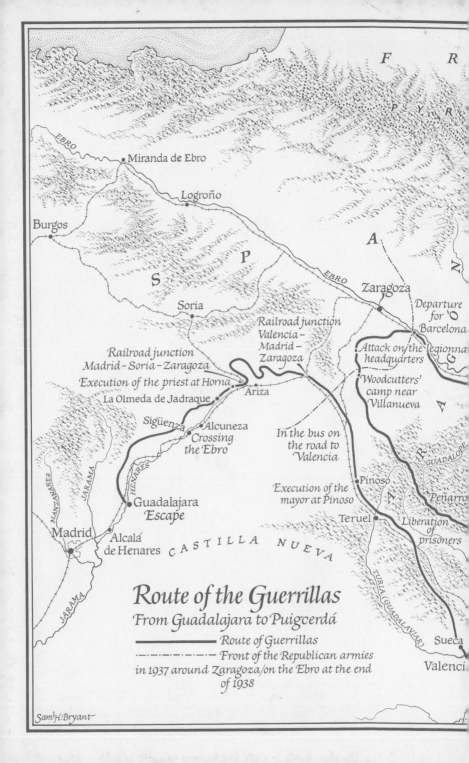

Route of the Guerrillas
From Guadalajara to Puigcerdá

———— Route of Guerrillas

—·—·— Front of the Republican armies
in 1937 around Zaragoza/on the Ebro at the end
of 1938

Sam¹ H. Bryant

FR
PYR
AN

Miranda de Ebro
Logroño
Burgos
EBRO
S   P
Soria
EBRO
Zaragoza
Departure
for
Barcelona

Railroad junction
Valencia–
Madrid–
Zaragoza

Attack on the legionna
headquarters

Railroad junction
Madrid–Soria–Zaragoza
Execution of the priest at Horna
La Olmeda de Jadraque
Ariza
Woodcutters'
camp near
Villanueva

Sigüenza
Alcuneza
Crossing
the Ebro

In the bus on
the road to
Valencia

A   R   A   G
GUADALOPE

Guadalajara
Escape

Execution of the
mayor at Pinoso

Pinoso
Peñarro

Liberation
of
prisoners

Madrid
Alcalá
de Henares

CASTILLA   NUEVA

Teruel

MANZANARES
JARAMA
HENARES

JARAMA

TURIA (GUADALAVIAR)

Sueca

Valenci